Martin Hawes is New Zealand's most popular financial author. This book on family trusts, first published in 1995 and revised many times since, has introduced the concept of trusts to over 130,000 people. Since then Martin has written a string of best-sellers on topics such as investment, mortgages, superannuation and tax.

Martin's background is in business and financial consultancy. As well as being a best-selling author of financial books, he has a number of independent, non-executive directorships. He is the chair of the Summer KiwiSaver Investment Committee, a director of Lifetime Income, and a board member of the New Zealand Shareholders' Association.

Martin is an Authorised Financial Adviser and his disclosure statement can be accessed free of charge at www.martinhawes. com. He lives in Christchurch and in his spare time he climbs mountains, rock-climbs, skis and cycles.

ALSO BY MARTIN HAWES

*Financial Secrets: The Complete New Zealand Guide to
  Everyday Finances* — revised edition 2011

*Letters to Aston: Lessons Learned from a Lifetime of
  Investments* — 2009

Investing for Twenty Good Summers — 2009

Property Investments: A Strategy for Success — revised
  edition 2008

*The School of Home Truths: Eight Lessons for Buying and
  Selling Property in New Zealand* — 2007

Family Trusts

THE MUST-HAVE NEW ZEALAND GUIDE

Martin Hawes

RANDOM HOUSE
NEW ZEALAND

RANDOM HOUSE

UK | USA | Canada | Ireland | Australia
India | New Zealand | South Africa | China

Random House is an imprint of the Penguin Random House group of companies, whose addresses can be found at global.penguinrandomhouse.com.

Penguin
Random House
New Zealand

First published 1995 by Shoal Bay Press, revised (7 times) and reprinted (19 times). This (9th) revised edition published 2020.

10 9 8 7 6 5 4 3 2 1

Book design by Megan van Staden and Cat Taylor © Penguin Random House New Zealand
Prepress by Image Centre Group
Printed and bound in Australia by Griffin Press, an Accredited ISO AS/NZS 14001 Environmental Management Systems Printer

A catalogue record for this book is available from the National Library of New Zealand.
ISBN 978-0-14-377530-0
eISBN 978-0-14-377531-7
penguin.co.nz

MIX
Paper | Supporting
responsible forestry
FSC® C018684

*This book is dedicated to my
three ultimate beneficiaries:
Golda, Greta and Hannah.*

*My sincere thanks to Stephen Brent
of RVG Law for his help
and advice with this book.*

Contents

Introduction

Kiwis Have Most Trusts

The first edition of this book was published over 25 years ago, and since its first publication in March 1995 the book has sold around 130,000 copies. This edition has been prompted by the enactment of the Trusts Act 2019 and a general decline in the benefit of family trusts. This Act, which will have a great impact on trusts in New Zealand, comes into effect on 30 January 2021.

A key theme of this book has always been a cost–benefit analysis of trusts. In every edition of the book I have tried to weigh up the advantages that might accrue from settling a trust against the disadvantages of doing so. When the book was first published in 1995 this was quite easy — for a great number of people the advantages of settling a trust greatly outweighed the disadvantages. Back in the 1990s there were many financial and family matters that could be greatly assisted by settling a family trust: superannuation surcharge, income tax, asset protection for residential care subsidies, death duties, and more latterly things like relationship property.

This led to New Zealand becoming the most 'over-trusted' country in the world. We have more family trusts in New Zealand per head of population than any other country. (By some counts there are 450,000 trusts in New Zealand, but there is no way of knowing whether this figure is accurate.)

Today many of the benefits of family trusts are either gone (with the superannuation surcharge and death duties having been abolished), or legislation has been enacted meaning that a trust is no longer effective in reducing the impact of certain matters (income tax changes). Moreover, case law seems to have been moving steadily against trusts, with the veil of a trust having been looked through in many court cases.

The scales of whether or not to have a trust have tipped. When you look at a cost–benefit analysis, it is no longer an easy matter to decide to settle (or continue) a trust, as the benefits are now smaller and the costs greater.

Perhaps the cost that has risen most is that of trust management. In previous editions of this book I have criticised the management of trusts in New Zealand, estimating that as many as 75 per cent of the trusts in New Zealand were so badly managed that they would not withstand scrutiny in a court. While I calculated this figure from only a relatively small number of trusts with which I had been close in my role as a financial adviser, many professionals in the field (lawyers and accountants) agreed with my rough assessment. In effect, many of the hundreds of thousands of trusts that are in New

Zealand have been managed as if the assets in them were still the belongings of the people who had settled the trust. The role of becoming a trustee was not taken particularly seriously, and in many cases there could be no certainty that a proper trust even existed. The effect of this has been that many trusts are sham trusts and could be overturned in court (and indeed many have been).

In the past, trusts have been extremely useful for people, and some trusts will continue to be so. Trusts have been used in such matters as succession planning, tax minimisation, getting around unpopular imposts, and for settling relationship property issues. However, successive governments have recognised that there has been revenue leakage from trusts, and there have been plenty of cases of people being treated unfairly because of a trust (particularly in the relationship property area). Legislative and case law have evolved accordingly. Changes to many of the things which concern trusts mean that it is now hard to imagine new taxes or other imposts that do not include some kind of anti-trust provision.

When the new Trusts Act comes into effect, it will place additional risk and costs on trusts, and so, because of the likely great impact of this, I have included a new chapter in this edition on the Act.

In many respects the Trusts Act does not make very much new law. In effect the Trusts Act instead reflects what should have been happening all along, especially in terms of the role and duties of trustees and how a trust should be managed. In fact, if New Zealand trusts had been managed as they should have been, there would not be a lot of the fuss which the Trusts Act is creating. Had people taken the position of trustee seriously and managed trusts as they should have, the Trusts Act would hardly have been necessary.

However, now, with the advent of the Trusts Act, along with changes to the rules surrounding residential care subsidies and income tax, it is a very good time to reconsider any trust you have settled. In fact, I believe that in the coming months there will be many professionals (lawyers, accountants and trust companies) sitting down with their clients to decide whether it is useful to continue the trust.

I think this is an extremely important conversation to have, and it is one that we should already have been having on a regular basis. This conversation will effectively mean undertaking a cost–benefit analysis: considering the likely future benefits of a trust against the weight of the costs that ownership of assets within a trust comes with. These costs cover not just financial cost, but also the cost of time that you will have to put in. Moreover, the Trusts Act has a requirement for disclosures to beneficiaries; that is, trustees have an obligation to give beneficiaries information about their trust. This disclosure in itself may well be very unattractive to people who have settled trusts, and it could also mean more disputes within families leading to more breach-of-trust litigation.

So while it has taken the Trusts Act to provoke a conversation on a wide scale, I think such conversations are nevertheless very useful. Moreover, I confidently predict many trusts will be wound up in the coming months and years as the implications of the changes to trusts and the full provisions of the Trusts Act are comprehended.

The cost–benefit analysis will see some people continue with the trusts that they have settled, in which case these people will need to ensure that the management of the trust is good, and that all trustees are taking their role as trustee seriously. Others will find, on analysis, that for them the scales have tipped, and the trust no longer offers enough benefit to counter the additional risk and cost, and so will bite the bullet and wind the trust up sooner rather than later. Yet there remain a number of good reasons for continuing with a trust. Some people will not want to wind up their trust because it is a useful device for succession planning, while others will want to continue with the trust because they are in business or the professions, and will want to be able to protect their assets for their families in the event of insolvency. There may also be people who continue with their trusts (or settle a trust) who are concerned about relationship property issues, although these people do need to take good advice before continuing with this. (In most cases it is better to consider a contracting-out agreement rather than the use of a family trust.)

I am not therefore predicting the demise of trusts as a whole: trusts have been around for centuries, and will no doubt be around for some centuries more. I am instead predicting the demise of some trusts (in fact, many trusts), as New Zealand has probably always had too many trusts. So it seems to be no bad thing that the Trusts Act will trigger a cleaning-out, and will encourage many people to wind up trusts they settled which no longer have good purpose or are too expensive to manage, given the benefits may now be limited.

In any event, people need to become better informed about trusts in general, and any trust that they have settled in particular. They will have to be careful to not fall between the devil and the deep blue sea and get the worst of both worlds — that is, to continue with a badly managed trust, thereby carrying the additional costs of the trust without the trust ultimately effecting its purpose. This has always seemed to me very much like insuring a property and then going out for the day leaving all the doors and windows wide open. To do that is to obviate the insurance policy; you still pay for the policy, but the policy will not be in effect.

This is therefore decision time: deciding whether you are still likely to benefit from a trust, and then either continuing with the trust, ensuring that it complies with the law, or winding it up. As I note in Chapter 6, winding up the trust will have a cost, but in winding it up now you may save yourself trouble and cost later. Therefore, take good advice and take your time to decide whether or not a trust is still right for you.

Martin Hawes

July 2020

I

What is a Family Trust and How Does it Work?

The principle is simple: you want to get rid of assets, to own less. Further, you want to do this by passing the assets on to someone else while retaining some control over them.

A family trust allows the ownership of some of your valuable assets to be in someone else's name, while you still have the use of them and some control over them.

To have a trust (any kind of trust, including a family trust), there must be three things that are certain:

— Certainty of **intention** — the settlor who is establishing the trust must intend to create a trust.

— Certainty of **subject matter** — the assets of the trust must be clearly identifiable.

— Certainty of **object** — the beneficiaries of the trust must be clearly defined.

The assets of a trust must be quite separate (and held separately) from the trustees' other personal assets. Ownership of the trust's assets goes into the name of the trustees. The trustees have the power to manage and deal with the assets according to the trust deed and the law of trusts.

ESTABLISHING A FAMILY TRUST

A family trust is established by drawing up and executing a trust deed. This document establishes the trust and sets out the way that the trust will be managed. It also specifies who, ultimately, will get the trust assets (i.e. the beneficiaries of the trust).

There are three parties involved in a family trust:

— **Settlor** — this is you, the person wishing to establish the trust by settling an asset on it.

— **Trustees** — these are the people who hold the ownership of the asset and look after it for the beneficiaries.

— **Beneficiaries** — these are the people who will ultimately get the assets or the benefit of them.

To establish a trust, a deed is executed whereby you, the settlor, transfer assets to the trust. With the repeal of gift duties in October 2011, this became a relatively simple process. Many people will now transfer assets completely to the trust, and as soon as this is done you no longer own the assets — the trust does.

The assets transferred into a trust are likely to be your most valuable assets — the family home, your business, investments, heirlooms and so on — assets you have worked all your life to obtain. In creating a trust, you are transferring ownership of your assets to another entity (the trust), one over which you will have some control, but not complete control. Clearly, this is not something to do without some serious thought.

Up until the repeal of gift duty, the transfer of assets into a trust was a much slower and more cumbersome process. Effectively settlors had to gift assets annually to the trust at the rate of $27,000 p.a. ($54,000 for a couple). This could take years, or even decades for those with large amounts of assets.

Now that gift duties have been repealed, no extended gifting is required — you can transfer whichever assets you choose directly into the trust. This means that you, as the settlor, transfer assets to the trustees, who hold and manage them for the beneficiaries. Diagrammatically, it looks like this:

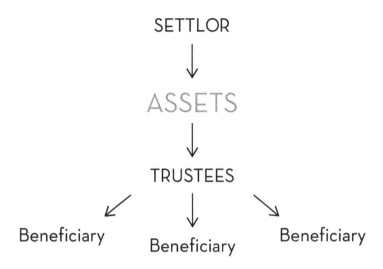

SETTLOR

↓

ASSETS

↓

TRUSTEES

↙ ↓ ↘

Beneficiary   Beneficiary   Beneficiary

To form a trust the settlor is handing over an asset to someone else (the trustee(s)), who will hold the asset for the benefit of someone else (the beneficiaries). If you think about this, you probably use simple trusts every day. For example, if you hire a car and forget to drop the keys back to the rental car company before your flight leaves, one of the airline staff might agree to take the keys back to the rental car company for you. You give her the keys and she duly drops them back. In accepting the keys from you, the airline staff member is acting in the role of trustee — she looks after the keys and gives them back to the rental car company (who, in this case, is the beneficiary). We do this kind of thing all of the time when we put someone into a position of trust with an asset.

Let's look at the different parties involved in a family trust in a bit more detail:

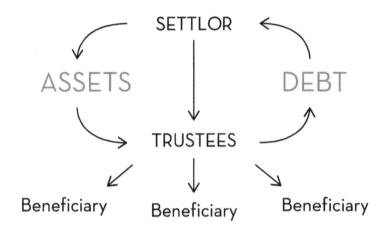

SETTLOR

If you are establishing the trust you are the settlor — it is said that you settle the trust. While this may seem straightforward enough, anyone who makes gifts to the trust can also be deemed to be the settlor. This stops people from getting a relative to settle the trust with, say, $20, so that they are not the settlor, but then transferring their assets to the trust and becoming a beneficiary. This practice was very common in Australia, but in New Zealand if you make gifts to the trust (as you certainly will at some point) you will be deemed to be the settlor.

APPOINTOR

Many trusts in New Zealand now have an appointor. This person has the right to appoint new trustees and beneficiaries, and so exercises considerable control over the trust.

Usually as settlor you are also appointor, although there are some risks with this (see the following section on trustees). Upon your death, the executor of your estate takes over the role of appointor unless you have nominated a new appointor under your will.

TRUSTEES

Trustees are the people who hold ownership of the assets you sell or gift to the trust. In owning the assets, the trustees can deal with them, control them, and sell them if they wish. They can decide (subject to the provisions of the trust deed) which beneficiaries will benefit from the trust and by how much. Trustees have duties, and these are now set out clearly in the Trusts Act (see Chapter 2). These duties must be performed, and a beneficiary may be able to bring an action for breach of trust if they are not. Agreeing to be a trustee of a family trust has always been a big step with plenty of risk. However, with the advent of the Trusts Act, the risk is even greater.

A family trust is usually discretionary, which means the trustees are given discretion over how the assets are dealt with. There is usually no requirement for trustees to bestow a benefit on any particular beneficiary in any particular proportion.

It is all at the trustees' discretion. The trustees could, if they chose, give a benefit to one of the children but nothing to the

REPEAL OF GIFT DUTIES

The abolition of gift duties as of 1 October 2011 brought in a range of issues and considerations. Some of them are:

— Most settlors of existing trusts will want to gift any remaining debt that is owed to them by the trust. However, if you have any concerns about your solvency or there are potential relationship issues, you should take advice on this point. It is possible in a minority of circumstances that gifting everything could create difficulties in the future.

— The gifting that you will probably want to do does not happen automatically. Some people believe that you do not need to do anything — that gifting just happens. It does not; you will need to sign a deed of gift, make a minute in the trust's minute book that a gift has been received, and adjust the trust's account (or asset register) accordingly. A call to your lawyer, accountant or trust professional is essential.

- No gift statement now needs to be sent to the IRD — you are able to gift as much as you want at any time.
- Annual gifting used to be the trigger for an annual meeting of trustees. Gifting may have been the initial reason for such a meeting, but most trusts also used the meeting to review the trust's affairs and its management. It is important that this still happens — for the majority of trusts, an annual meeting is the first step to ensure that the trust is well managed.
- Various government agencies and others (such as lawyers involved in relationship issues or insolvency) have been taking a very close look at how trusts are administered following the repeal of gift duty. For example, the Ministry of Social Development (MSD) is taking a very hard line regarding eligibility for benefits (including rest-home subsidies) when gifting to a trust has taken place. Where there has been gifting of over $27,000 p.a. (whether for a couple or an individual), the MSD is likely to decline a rest-home subsidy.

other two, even if all of the children are beneficiaries. This may sound unfair in terms of your family, and such a thing is most unlikely to happen. However, the discretionary nature of the trust is a very important aspect of family trusts, as shall be seen later. At this stage you should recognise that the trusts that you settle will operate at the complete discretion of the trustees — making theirs a very important role.

SPECIAL TRUST ADVISER

The Trusts Act has made provision for a new role in trusts called a 'special trust adviser'. This is someone who is appointed to advise on any trust matter, and it seems likely that many of them will be investment or financial advisers.

Trustees do not have to follow the advice of a special trust adviser, but if they do follow such advice a subsequent breach of trust charge is far less likely to be upheld.

CONTROL OVER TRUSTEES

From what we have just learned above, obviously the choice of trustees is critical. Having sold your assets into the trust, you have, in a legal sense at least, 'alienated' yourself from them — you no longer own them. In order for you to retain the use and control of those assets and for them to end up where you want them to, it is critical that you, as settlor, have some mechanism of control over the trustees.

This can be done in a number of ways. Most importantly, you can reserve to yourself the right (as appointor) both to fire existing trustees and to hire new ones. This right, clearly spelled out in the trust deed, will give you a large measure of control over the trustees, and therefore over the assets the trustees hold. However, it should be said that taking such power as appointor may give you so much control that there is some risk in the future of having your trust voided as a sham. Someone attacking the trust could claim that, because you hold all of the control, the trust is really just you in another guise.

The second way in which you can exercise some control over the trustees is to be a trustee yourself. There is nothing to stop the settlor of a trust also being a trustee.

What I do not recommend, however, is for the settlor to be sole trustee. While there is nothing necessarily illegal about this at the moment, I think it is wise to have at least one other trustee to make the arrangement an arm's-length transaction. If you are the settlor and the sole trustee you are in effect selling or gifting assets to yourself, which gives at least the appearance of a sham transaction. Even being the settlor and also one of, say, two trustees may cause difficulties in the future. Although this sort of arrangement is within existing law at present, it is quite possible that changes tightening the law on trusts may affect trusts where the parties are too close. These changes could come from Parliament or through judge-made law.

The third way to exert some control over the trustees is to have drawn up a 'letter of wishes' (sometimes called a 'memorandum of wishes'). This document records your wishes as settlor at the time the trust is established or at any future time. It may include such things as the proportion that each of the beneficiaries should receive from the trust, or a request that particular assets not be sold, or perhaps that a certain beneficiary not receive anything unless a certain event (say, a graduation) takes place.

These wishes are just that: they are merely your desires, and, unlike the provisions within the trust deed, do not bind the trustees. But if they are stated in a document attached to the trust deed, they will most certainly carry weight when the trustees are making their decisions.

The fourth way that control may be exerted is for you to maintain a situation whereby the trust continues to owe you some money. This was common before the repeal of gift duties. In such a scenario, you would establish a trust with a very small asset (say, $20) and then sell valuable assets to the trust, which would fund the purchase by borrowing from you, the settlor. This debt owed to you would slowly be gifted to the trust over a good number of years. In most instances, at any particular time the trust that you had settled would owe you money, which would give you rights as a creditor to demand repayment. This would exert some pressure on the trustees, who might otherwise have been refusing to do what you as settlor wanted. This continues to be a reason for some people not to gift all of their assets to the trust straight away, even though gift duties have been repealed.

The fifth and most telling means of exerting control over the trustees is to appoint good trustees in the first place. The trustees you appoint will hold 'your' assets. You therefore need trustees who will be sympathetic to you.

ADVISORY TRUSTEE

Many trusts now have an 'advisory trustee', who is usually the settlor. The advisory trustee does not have the rights and responsibilities of a trustee, but must be consulted (or advised) before the trustees enter into any major transaction.

This allows you as settlor to stay involved with the trust while not being a trustee. It would allow you to act to remove trustees if they were about to enter into any transaction that you did not wish them to.

CHOOSING TRUSTEES

Choosing the trustees is your most important act in forming a trust. After all, these people are going to own what were once your most valuable assets.

'Trust' is the operative word here: you want people you can trust. And not just trust to do what you and your family wish, but trust in terms of their ability and competence.

Your choice of trustees will depend on what the trust is likely to own and what it is likely to do. For example, if the trust is established simply to own the family home, you will not need trustees with as great a degree of skill as if the trust is set up to own and manage large and complex investments.

If you expect the trust to carry on after your death (perhaps because you want certain assets to stay in the family, or your children are young and will not receive major benefits until they have grown up), you might look at choosing different trustees from those you would choose if you want the trust's assets to be distributed immediately after your death. A trustee company is a good idea if you want the trust to continue, because it is a permanent entity.

Anyone can be a trustee, provided they are *sui juris* (over 18 years of age and of normal mental capacity). They may be individuals ('natural persons' is the quite amusing legal term) or corporates — a company can be a trustee. However, you will probably not want to appoint a company as sole trustee if you control that company. This is because, as mentioned above, this gives you full legal control over the trust and creates the impression of a possible sham transaction.

There is no legal limit to the number of trustees you can have. However, most trusts have two or three, with few having more. Having more than two or three trustees can create practical and logistical difficulties, particularly when they are all required to sign documents or agree to a particular transaction.

Similarly, very few trusts will have only one trustee, although again there is no legal bar to this. The major problem with having a sole trustee is that there are no checks and balances on that person's performance, and no easy transition if this trustee dies or gives up the role suddenly. There can also be difficulties if the trustee is away or ill and not available to sign an essential document. The trust is then effectively hamstrung until the trustee's return.

Most people appoint themselves as a trustee as they want to see that the trust is managed according to their wishes. If you are married or living with someone, both of you should be trustees (assuming that the assets belong to both of you). This is to ensure that, in the case of a matrimonial or relationship break-up, you both have control. In addition, in my view, one of the trustees should be a professional (see page 32).

Appointing trustees to act after you have died (or if you become disabled or do not want to be a trustee) needs a lot of thought. This is most important if you have young children — in this case, the trustees are going to continue to hold assets for years or even decades, and they will have to exercise their discretion. Assuming that you are going to have at least two trustees (as in most cases), you should aim to appoint one of each of the following types of trustee.

— Either yourself or a close personal friend or family member. The purpose of having a long-standing, trusted family member or friend is to ensure you have at least one trustee who is sympathetic to you, knows how you think, and is most likely always to act with your best interests at heart. In the event that you are away (or if you have died), when a decision needs to be made then you have someone who should be able to represent you faithfully. There is always a danger here that you will fall out with this family member or friend over something. Should this happen, you then have someone not very friendly at all dealing with 'your' assets — assets over which you want control. However, provided you have inserted in your trust deed the right to fire trustees, this should not be too much of a problem.

— A professional. This is someone who knows how trusts

work. It may be a lawyer, an accountant, a trust company or a financial adviser. It is someone who will ensure that all documents and records are filed in a safe place and that the trust minute book is kept up to date.

A PROFESSIONAL AS TRUSTEE

By having a knowledgeable professional as one of the trustees you can make sure that all of the trustees comply with the trust deed and the law. It may be that, if the trust is buying or selling a major asset, more specialist legal or accounting advice will be needed. However, this would also be the case if you were buying or selling something yourself. For most trusts owning, say, the family home and some investments, a professional as a trustee should ensure that everything is properly managed.

The question of who to choose as a professional trustee is a difficult one, though. Not only does this person need to be well educated or trained in trust law (at least in the broad sense, if not in the very fine detail), he or she also needs to have some knowledge of you as a person and have sympathy with your aims for the trust.

Some of my worst experiences (fortunately not many!) with family trusts have been where a professional as trustee has taken his position so seriously that he has insisted on scrutinising every minor detail before agreeing to a transaction.

Common sense is the order of the day, and if you are in doubt or know no one with the appropriate skills you will probably not go far wrong by appointing one of the permanent trustee companies. The staff of these companies are well trained in all aspects of trusts and will be able to advise on everything from the drafting of your trust deed to taxation.

One problem with having a professional as trustee is that you are likely to be charged for his or her services. The charge will vary according to what the trust owns, what it does, whether many transactions are required and the individual professional's charging policy. If, for example, the trust owns only the family home, professional charges will be small. On the other hand, if you have a trading trust owning major business assets with a lot of transactions, the charges could run to many thousands of dollars.

The important thing is that you know the basis for charging. It may be difficult for a trustee to give you an estimate of likely costs until the trust has been running for a while, but if you at least know whether the charge will be based on an hourly rate or a percentage of the trust's assets you may avoid considerable difficulty later.

TRUSTEES AS OWNERS

Once you have appointed your trustees (typically yourself and a professional or trustee company), the assets you are placing in trust will be put into their names. This means they will become the registered owners. In the case of the family home (or other property), the names of your trustees will appear on the title. Anyone searching to find out who a property or a company 'belongs' to will find only the names of the trustees — not the 'beneficial' owners.

Often a search of a property will disclose two names as the

registered owners. No mention is made on the property title (nor often on share registers) that these people are holding the property in trust for others. This ultimately makes the ownership confidential — no one can find out who is behind the trust — which is very attractive to those who wish to have their business or financial affairs removed from the public eye. Unlike companies, there is no public register for trusts where the beneficiaries and other details are recorded (although the Law Commission was considering this at one stage).

However, while the assets are held in the trustees' names, so too are the liabilities. Thus if there is a mortgage on the trust's property, that mortgage shows the trustees' names as the borrowers. This could, of course, create a problem in that the trustees can become personally liable for the trust's borrowings and debt.

This difficulty is relieved by inserting a clause in the trust's mortgage document (or other loan agreement) stating that any independent trustees' liability is limited to the assets of the trust. An independent trustee is a trustee who is not entitled to benefit from the trust — for example, a professional trustee such as a solicitor or an accountant. By inserting this clause (obviously with the approval of the lender) you ensure that the trustees cannot be pursued personally in the event that the trust becomes insolvent. The lender may want a personal guarantee from someone (most probably from you, the settlor).

However, there are other liabilities the trust may incur that may affect the trustees personally. Unless there is explicit agreement between the trust and the creditor (the person who is owed money) that any liability is limited to the assets of the trust, the debt could well become a personal debt.

Unpaid taxes fall into this category. Trustees can be pursued personally by the Inland Revenue Department (IRD) for any taxes the trust does not or cannot pay. The situation is similar as regards debts to others (such as tradespeople or professional fees) where there is not a clear agreement to limit liability.

BENEFICIARIES

The beneficiaries are those who will eventually benefit from the trust. These will usually be children, grandchildren, wider family members, or perhaps a close family friend or a charity. The beneficiaries must be due the 'natural love and affection' of the settlor. If they are not, the forgiveness of debt by gifting may come under the accrual rules. These rules mean that when a debt is forgiven, the amount of the forgiven debt becomes taxable income for the trust.

Most typically the beneficiaries will be members of your family — people you want to benefit from the assets you have placed in trust. Some trusts specify that some beneficiaries will receive only income from the trust while others may receive both income and capital. It would be wise to have this sort of personal requirement recorded in the trust deed.

It is most important that the beneficiaries are not a closed group — you must ensure (in the trust deed) that more beneficiaries may be added later. You may choose to add particular named individuals or specify that they may be added 'naturally'; for example, if the beneficiaries are your children or grandchildren, and are referred to as a class (rather than named), and another is born, that child automatically becomes a beneficiary.

If the beneficiaries were a closed group, they could, on reaching the age of 18, 'gang up' and require the trust be wound up, the assets sold and the proceeds distributed.

Beneficiaries as such have very few rights. It must be remembered that a family trust is discretionary, meaning the trustees have absolute discretion as to which beneficiary will benefit, when and by what amount. Under the Trusts Act, beneficiaries have a right to information but no right to a benefit.

A beneficiary who misses out has no claim against the trust and cannot bring an action against it. The only exception to this would be if the trustees had failed to consider a beneficiary entirely. Aside from such very limited instances, the trustees can distribute whatever they like to whomever they like.

There is nothing to stop you being a beneficiary of your own trust, although before estate duties were abolished 30 years ago this was not possible. However, you should think carefully about this. Legislative changes over time, and any future changes the government may make, are likely to be aimed first at trusts where the parties are very close (or, indeed, the same).

Similarly, depending on the purpose of your trust, a separation of the parties is desirable so that an arm's-length transaction is maintained. The important thing is alienation of assets: that there is true removal of you as the beneficial owner in favour of some other group as the beneficial owner. While you may be one member of that group, it may prove better over time if you are not. Do not forget, however, that although initially you may not be named as a beneficiary, as appointor you will probably have the right in future to name further beneficiaries, one of whom may be yourself.

ASSETS

A family trust can own anything — excluding people, slavery being illegal in this country!

A family trust can own real estate, shares (in both listed and private companies), unit trusts, government stock, interest-bearing deposits, life insurance policies, family heirlooms, art, jewellery, the family racehorse, business assets, debts on loans, and so on.

Obviously what the trust does purchase depends on you and your intentions. Some people, for example, want only to protect the family home, while others wish to establish a trading trust to carry on their business. Still other people will want to place in trust all of their assets, including perhaps commercial property, shares and other investments as well as their lifestyle assets (such as their home, holiday home, boat and timeshare unit).

The choice here is very personal and depends entirely on what you are trying to achieve. Nevertheless, be aware that the trustees must invest the trust's assets prudently; someone could claim that the trust's ownership of a Toyota Corolla is not prudent investing. If the trust wants to own this car it would be better to document clearly that it is being purchased and used by one of the beneficiaries as a benefit, rather than being purchased as an investment.

Similarly, if the trust only owns the family home, someone attacking the trust could claim that the trustees had not acted prudently because they had not properly diversified. Some trust deeds have a clause allowing such undiversified investments (often called an 'eccentric investment clause') which seems to me to be a very wise addition to the trust deed and becomes necessary with the advent of the Trusts Act.

This is a brief overview of a typical trust arrangement.

There are three very important things to keep in mind:

— The trust is **discretionary**; the discretion is in the hands of the trustees, and you should therefore be very careful as to whom you appoint to act both while you are alive and after you have gone.

— The trustees must act **prudently and fairly**.

— When you have sold the assets into the trust **you no longer own them** — the trust does. You may be a trustee and you may still enjoy the use of the assets (e.g. the family home), but you are no longer the sole beneficial owner, and therefore you have to act as trustee and bear in mind your duties and that there are other beneficiaries.

FORMATION OF THE TRUST

A trust is now quite simple to form. The abolition of gift duty has simplified the arrangement, making fewer transactions necessary.

In the past, a trust was formed by the settlor putting a very small asset into a trust (perhaps $20) and then selling other more valuable assets into the trust. The trust borrowed from the settlor, which created a debt that was then gifted at the rate of $27,000 p.a. (the greatest amount you could gift without attracting gift duties). This is covered in more detail below.

With repeal of gift duty, the formation of a trust became more simple. The trust is created with the deed, and any assets that you choose, regardless of value, can be transferred to the trust. This means that the day the trust is formed, it owns completely anything that you want it to own — the house, business, investments, family heirlooms and so on.

There is no longer a need to gift over years or even decades — it can all be done immediately. What were once your assets are instantly the trust's assets; you no longer own them. However, be aware that the MSD looks at gifting when considering an application for a residential care subsidy, and declines these applications where there has been gifting over $27,000 p.a. Similarly, there is law covering gifting to avoid creditors, i.e. if someone makes gifts and shortly afterwards is bankrupted, the Official Assignee may try to wind back such gifts.

The aim of a family trust is for you to own less; possibly nothing at all. This was not practicable immediately when there were gift duties, as when the assets were sold to the trust you may not have owned the assets but you still owned a debt (the one that the trust owed to you). Now, on the day that the trust is formed, everything that you own can be out of your name and into the trust's ownership. It looks like this:

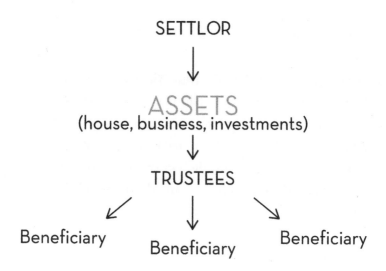

Clearly, the ability to instantly move assets from your ownership to the trust's creates some public policy issues. Can insolvent people quickly push their assets off to a trust one day and then be declared bankrupt the next? Can people transfer assets to a trust on Tuesday and then on Wednesday apply for a rest-home subsidy? The answer in brief is 'no' — it is not as easy as that. As we shall see later (Chapter 3), there is legislation that controls these kinds of things. Moreover, various agencies like the Official Assignee (in the case of insolvency) or the MSD (in the case of rest-home subsidies) will be developing rules regarding the interpretation of their respective legislation and working out how these rules will be applied. This will no doubt become apparent as the Trusts Act comes into effect.

Nevertheless, with the repeal of gift duties, it is now much easier to move assets to a trust. There is no gradual gifting —

assets immediately go out of your name and into the trust's. With the ability to gift everything immediately, this takes all assets out of your name completely on day one (assuming that is what you want).

Gifting everything is, of course, a double-edged sword: it does mean that you will own nothing and be completely at the mercy of the trustees. As discussed earlier, this should not be too much of a problem as there are ways to retain some control over the trust (not the least of which is you being a trustee). Nevertheless, many people who had settled a trust felt more secure and had more control when they were owed substantial amounts by the trust.

Those who are settling trusts — or, indeed those who have already settled a trust but have not yet completed gifting — need to think whether it might be wise to leave some debt owing to them. This may be useful to maintain more control over the trust, but also because some people still want to have some form of asset in their own names. I suspect that the majority of people will want to have everything in the trust, but there may be a few who want assets in their own name. Moreover, as mentioned, both the MSD and the Official Assignee do not like to see large gifts being made.

With this in mind, it is worth reviewing how trusts were established before the repeal of gift duties.

Remember that the object of the trust is always for you to own less (possibly nothing at all). A trust would be formed, a deed signed and a very small asset (usually $20) would be put into the trust to start it. Diagrammatically it looked like this:

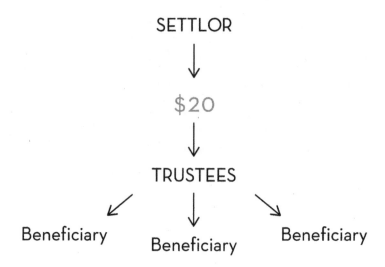

SETTLOR

↓

$20

↓

TRUSTEES

↙   ↓   ↘

Beneficiary   Beneficiary   Beneficiary

However, there was a problem here. The trust has only the $20 with which to purchase your assets, and no bank or financier is likely to lend the trust 100 per cent of the value of the family home, let alone 100 per cent of the value of shares or an investment property. How then did the trust fund the purchase of these valuable assets?

The answer was for you, the settlor and the previous owner of the assets, to *lend* the trust the money to buy your own assets — a sort of vendor-finance arrangement.

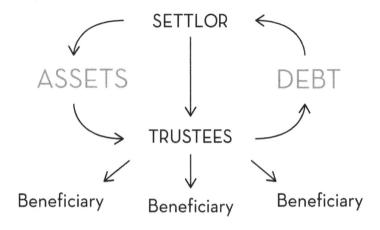

You could not simply give your property to the trust, as there were limits on gifting.

So, as you have seen in the second diagram, the asset had been sold to the trust, funded by a debt back to you. In effect you had swapped the asset that you owned (say, the family home) for a debt from the trustees to the same value.

However, since the aim is to own less, this arrangement had still not really got you very far. You had simply swapped assets — instead of owning a house you now owned a house-sized debt. Your overall wealth had remained the same.

This debt could be dealt with by gifting at the rate of $27,000 p.a. ($54,000 p.a. for a couple), which could take years (even decades) to complete. At any time while the gifting process was happening, you still owned the ungifted portion of the debt;

that is, you still had a significant asset in your name. Generally, this would defeat the purpose of why you had settled the trust.

Now, as noted above, all of the gifting can be done on day one if that is what you want. No debt needs to be created at the beginning: your assets are simply transferred out of your name and into the trust's, and, with the signing of the deed, it is all done. As already noted, there may be people who want to retain some debt, in which case the trust will continue to owe an amount to them. However, if you want to own nothing, it is now very quick and easy to do so.

THE TRUST DEED

The deed is the document that establishes the trust and records its terms. Although it is possible to have a trust without a deed, it is not advisable.

The deed may be only two or three pages long, or it may run to 50 or 60 pages. Many legal and accounting firms have their own form of deed on their computers, and can quickly and efficiently incorporate your specific personal requirements.

Generally, the length of the deed and its particular form are not important, but I believe that as a matter of good practice the deed should be worded in plain English that a layperson can understand. Some of the more old-fashioned deeds may be written in legal jargon and contain terms that many people do not understand, but there has been a trend away from this in recent years. I firmly believe you should not sign anything you do not understand, and a family trust deed is no exception. The deed establishes who may be trustees, the powers of the trustees, what they may invest in, and who will be the beneficiary or beneficiaries. Often much space will be given to specifying what the trustees may invest in and how they may apply the trust's funds. Effectively the deed establishes that the trustees are able to do nearly anything they deem prudent with the funds.

The deed also records the trustees' powers, which are very wide. A typical clause might go something like this: '. . . their power is absolute and uncontrolled and every power vested in them shall be exercised in their absolute and uncontrolled discretion . . .'

That just about says it all!

Once you have executed the deed you can alter it only with difficulty and in exceptional circumstances, unless the deed includes a specific power of variation or a power of resettlement. If there is no power of variation, any change would almost certainly require the sanction of the High Court, and there would need to be some most unusual reason or circumstances to convince the court to allow a change.

I personally have never seen a trust deed altered, but it should be noted that most modern trust deeds empower the trustees to resettle the trust's property onto a new trust. This is far more practical and efficient than approaching the High Court.

COMMON CLAUSES

Some of the common clauses found in trust deeds require comment:

— There is usually power given to the settlor to remove existing trustees and appoint new ones. This is important as a means of control over the trust. Similarly, the settlor is empowered to remove beneficiaries and appoint new ones. This may be important if you do not wish the class of beneficiaries to be fixed.

— In many trust deeds there is a clause stipulating that these powers shall be vested in the appointor (who is almost always the settlor). However, upon the death (or incapacitation) of the settlor, the appointor may be somebody nominated by the settlor, or be the executor of the settlor's estate. Given that the appointor has the most practical as well as technical control over the trust, the choice of any other person for this role requires careful consideration.

— There is nearly always a clause in the trust deed indemnifying the trustees from actions that they may take as trustees. The exception to any indemnity would be in the case of fraud or negligence.

— Most trust deeds require any decision made by the trust to be unanimous. If you as settlor are a trustee, too, this effectively gives you a right of veto. But this provision is a double-edged sword, because another trustee could also refuse to sanction something you propose.

— Some trusts specifically exclude particular potential beneficiaries, perhaps for family reasons. When estate duties were in force it was a requirement under the Estate and Gift Duties Act 1968 that the settlor be specifically excluded from having any benefit under the trust. Although it no longer applies, there are people who still adhere to this rule through a fear of the return of estate duties (which is very unlikely in my view).

— The vesting day is the date of the winding up of the trust and the distribution of its assets to the final beneficiaries. This must always be within 125 years of the trust's formation (which should see us all long gone). Most trusts do not survive for anything like this time, and there can be any number of other triggers for bringing forward the vesting day. Many trust deeds give discretion to the trustees as to when the vesting day should be. Most typically it is on the death of the settlor. Other reasons would be the marriage or a particular birthday (such as the thirtieth) of a beneficiary, or perhaps the separation or divorce of the settlor.

— Most modern trust deeds have a clause allowing the trustees to resettle the trust's assets on another trust. This is a practical way of changing the terms of a trust, as mentioned previously, although it cannot be used as a way of adding new beneficiaries to a trust.

Q Can you be settlor, trustee and a beneficiary of a trust?

A The answer is simple and complex at the same time. The simple answer is that under existing law there is nothing to stop you being all three. Indeed, there are many trusts in New Zealand where the settlor is also a trustee and a beneficiary.

There are advantages in being all three — being a trustee of your own trust gives you a greater measure of control, and being a beneficiary allows you the use and benefit of the assets of the trust.

For death duties purposes, under the Estate and Gift Duties Act 1968 you used not to be able to be a beneficiary of a trust you had settled. This meant that if you were not specifically excluded as a beneficiary, the trust's assets could be taken into the estate duty calculation. Of course, death duties were abolished years ago, but it is useful, nevertheless, to remember that in the distant past there was anti-trust legislation, and to bear in mind that something like this could return in the future.

However, having said that you can be all three, there is always the worry that there will be some law change (either through Parliament or a court ruling) that will adversely affect such trusts. I am particularly cautious and conservative on this: I believe any attack on trusts is likely to be aimed at trusts where the parties are too close.

Many trust advisers say that if there is such a change in law you could use the resettlement clause in the trust deed to resettle the trust onto a new, more convenient trust. They are probably right. Nevertheless, I think you should assume as little control over the trust as you are comfortably able to do.

2

The Trusts Act

The Trusts Act comes into effect on 30 January 2021, but has already set the cat amongst the pigeons in the world of family trusts. In reality, the Trusts Act doesn't change the law a great deal, and, in the view of one law firm at least, is regarded as an evolution of the law rather than a revolution. In fact, the Trusts Act effectively codifies a great deal of common law (judge-made law) and legislation that already exists.

The Trusts Act sets out the duties of trustees very clearly, and in doing so brings together a number of parts of the law so that, as far as possible, we have trust management all in one place. I do not think that the Trusts Act will mean that there is no more litigation on trusts — in fact, there could be even more as interpretations and clarifications are sought. Nevertheless, the Act does make the law more accessible and is quite readable for a non-lawyer, which is in contrast with some of the judgments that are used as precedents.

The Act repeals the Perpetuities Act 1964 and the Trustee Act 1956, and in doing so changes the length of time that a trust can last: its possible lifetime is now 125 years instead of 80 years. The Act also changes the age of a majority — an adult is now someone who is over 18 years (rather than the previous 20 years). However, it is in the areas of the poor standard of governance and administration of trusts, along with the high levels of settlor control and conflicts of interest, that the Act really takes aim. The clear statements of required management, and the rules for disclosure of information to beneficiaries, will give cause for many who have settled trusts to rethink.

In some ways the Trusts Act simply sets out best practice for trust management. However, as many trusts have not adopted best practice for the management of their assets and in dealing with the beneficiaries, these trusts will need to make some big changes. For many, these changes will be a step too far.

In fact, most of the duties of a trustee and the management of trusts were already part of the law, but the codification as set out in the Trusts Act makes this clearer, and as such has been a trigger for people to revisit the original reason for forming a trust. The question of whether to form a trust or not has effectively been turned on its head; previously the question was why would you not form a trust, whereas now the question is why would you have a trust.

Already, in anticipation of the new Act coming into force, far more existing trusts are being terminated than new ones formed, and this trend is certain to continue apace. The codification and clear setting out of the duties of trustees, and the management that is required of a good trust, make things very clear to settlors and trustees who have not been managing a trust properly. Moreover, by clearly putting down in black and white the trustees' duties of disclosure to beneficiaries, the Act invites disgruntled beneficiaries to 'have a go'. It seems to me that beneficiaries are much more likely to act against any breach of trust, and so litigation is therefore most unlikely to reduce with the passing of this Act. In fact, it will almost certainly increase.

There are therefore far greater risks for trustees (as they are more likely to be involved in disputes and litigation), which means that, in general, they will take their roles much more seriously than previously — they will simply have to. Trustees are personally liable in many cases, and this now includes directors of companies that act as trustees. This added burden of trusteeship will mean that prospective trustees will be very careful before taking up the position, and, if they do take up the position of trustee, will put a great deal more time, effort and energy into their role. This in turn will lead to increased costs for trusts.

The rules for disclosure to beneficiaries are also set down in the Trusts Act. The Act makes it very clear that beneficiaries need certain basic information regarding a trust of which they are a beneficiary, and this will further put people off trusts.

All of this, along with the gradual erosion of some of the rationales for trusts (such as tax minimisation and minimising estate duties), may see a stampede to the door. Many people will want to get out of their trust and wind it up, but it seems to me that the legal profession in particular has been rather slow in advising their clients. Many trusts that should be terminated will not be wound up before the Act comes into force. Of course, the timing on this is probably not too important (for most people it would not matter whether or not the trust was wound up a little before the implementation of the Act or a little after), but I think 2021 will be a busy time for lawyers winding up trusts.

The Act has several main features, and some of these are outlined below. The purpose of the Act is to set out the core principles of the law relating to trusts and to make this law more accessible to people. The Act is written in (reasonably) plain English, and I would encourage anyone who has settled a trust or who is a trustee to read it. The main features of the Act are as follows.

DUTIES OF TRUSTEES

The Act sets out two groups of duties: mandatory duties and default duties.

MANDATORY DUTIES

Mandatory duties are those which have to be performed and cannot be modified or excluded by the terms of the trust. There are five of these, and there is no way out; you have to do them:

1. a duty to know the terms of the trust

2. a duty to act in accordance with the terms of the trust

3. a duty to act honestly and in good faith

4. a duty to act for the benefit of the beneficiaries

5. a duty to exercise powers for proper purpose.

All trustees of family trusts will need to keep these five mandatory duties in mind when managing the trust. A trustee simply must carry out these duties and manage the trust in accordance with them.

DEFAULT DUTIES

There are 10 default duties, and trustees must perform each of these duties unless it is modified or excluded by the terms of the trust. The default duties are:

1. to exercise a general duty of care

2. to invest prudently

3. to not exercise a power for own benefit

4. to actively and regularly consider the exercise of powers

5. to not bind or commit trustees to any future exercise of discretion

6. to avoid a conflict of interest

7. to act impartially

8. to not profit from the trusteeship

9. to act for no reward

10. to act unanimously.

It is critical to note that these default duties can be modified by the trust deed itself. A good example of this is the duty to invest prudently. Imagine a trust (like many in New Zealand) which owns nothing but the family home, which is valued at $1 million. This is a common situation, where the settlors have decided that they want to protect the family home in the event of their business becoming insolvent, for example. However, from a trust point of view, a case could be made that the trustees, in simply owning a family home, have not diversified the funds in the trust. A prudent trustee, thinking of the best deployment of the $1 million he or she is managing, would sell the family home and invest that money in a diversified portfolio. Clearly the trustees, by continuing to own just a family home, have breached the duty of prudence by concentrating all of the trust funds on just one asset.

Of course, in such a case a diversified portfolio was never the intention of the settlors (you can't live in a diversified portfolio). And so here it would be wise for the trust deed to include a clause allowing for 'eccentric' investment strategies; that is, to allow the ownership simply of the family home with no diversification. It is likely many trusts in New Zealand currently do not have a clause allowing for 'eccentric' investment strategies, and an amendment to their trust deed may be required so that such a clause can be inserted.

There will be many instances where people will want to 'contract out' of the Act's default duties via the trust deed. This will mean that trusts will need to be carefully reviewed, and, where the family decides to continue with the trust, alterations may be made to the deed (or perhaps the trust resettled). This could be difficult where older trust deeds are being used with no power of resettlement or no power of alteration. This will require good and careful legal advice, and, possibly, the approval of all of the beneficiaries.

RECORD-KEEPING

The Trusts Act gives trustees an obligation to keep good records. Section 45 of the Trusts Act sets out these and includes such items as:

— the trust deed

— any variations to the trust deed

— a record of trust property that identifies assets

— records of any liabilities and expenses

— records of trustee decisions

— contracts

— accounting records

— letter of wishes

— documents of appointment

— records of the removal and discharge of trustees.

These documents must be kept for the life of the trust, and each trustee must keep a copy of these records. As you would expect, trustees are required to pass on those documents to the incoming trustee(s) when their trusteeship ends.

This requirement to keep records is nothing new — any good trustees (in fact, anyone in business or in a position of responsibility) will want to keep good records of what they are doing. However, the Act, again, sets out and codifies this record-keeping. In the event that a beneficiary brings a claim for breach of trust, this means there will be little debate regarding whether record-keeping was up to scratch or not — the requirements are set down in black and white.

DISCLOSURE TO BENEFICIARIES

Perhaps the most controversial part of the Act is the sections that require trustees to give information to beneficiaries. These requirements will need to be given a great deal of thought by people who have formed trusts with particular respect to their own family circumstances.

The Act requires basic information to be given to beneficiaries as a matter of course. First is a requirement that a beneficiary will need to be told that he/she is in fact a beneficiary. This will come as a surprise to some beneficiaries within some families, as they may not even know of the existence of the trust. There is no ambiguity now. Beneficiaries have to be told that they are beneficiaries, and are therefore entitled to some basic information.

This basic trust information that must be given is:

— notification that the beneficiary is, in fact, a beneficiary

— the name and contact details of the trustees

— notification of the appointment, removal and retirement of trustees as they occur

— the right of the beneficiary to request a copy of the trust deed or other trust information.

There are some exemptions for giving this information — in fact, there is a long list of exemptions, some of which are extremely general and will, no doubt, be the subject of litigation within families where there has been a falling-out. These include:

— whether the information has personal or commercial confidentiality

— the age and circumstances of the beneficiary

— the effect on the beneficiary of giving the information

— the effect of giving the information on relationships within the family

— the nature and context of any request for any information.

As you can see, some of these will require judgement, and the exercise of that judgement could lead to dispute. However, although there are these exemptions, it has to be remembered that under the Act, trustees will have to give basic information (which includes the beneficiaries being told that they can request other information), and I suspect that these disclosures will cause some angst within some families. Not all families enjoy happy relations at all times, and there will no doubt be some disgruntled members who use the information gained to stir up mischief.

AGE OF MAJORITY

Up until the advent of the Trusts Act, an adult was defined as somebody 20 years of age or more.

Under the Trusts Act, this changes to 18 years of age, and means that beneficiaries of both trusts and wills are able to benefit from age 18.

SPECIAL TRUST ADVISER

A trust may now appoint someone called a 'special trust adviser', and the process for appointing such a person is set out in the Act. The appointment of a special trust adviser will probably be required in a range of different circumstances where there is a gap in the skill set of existing trustees — for example, investment skills.

A special trust adviser is not a trustee: their role is advisory, rather than having any fiduciary duty.

Trustees do not have to follow the advice from a special trust adviser, but where they do, trustees will be protected from a trust breach if they have acted on the adviser's recommendation. Large trusts, in particular those with complicated investment portfolios, may well think enlisting a special trust adviser is a good idea.

In the past many trustees were advised not to record the reasons for some of their decisions. However, if a trust has a special trust adviser it would be a good idea to record that the trustees' actions were in accordance with advice received from that special trust adviser. This is because section 127 of the Trusts Act puts the onus on trustees to establish that what they have done was reasonable. Following the advice of a trust adviser would be considered a reasonable course of action in the vast majority of cases.

3

The Benefits of a Family Trust

Family trusts (or at least the idea of putting assets into someone else's name) have been around since Roman times. Back then, senators used trusts to circumvent laws they found inconvenient. The law may have been different in those days, but the intent was much the same — to own less (or to at least appear to own less) than what you had use and control over. In some ways the reasons for forming a family trust are still much the same.

It is possible to identify at least a dozen reasons why people form a family trust: in fact, the reasons are as many as the number of trusts formed. It is a very personal and individual thing.

Because of their discretionary and flexible nature, trusts can often achieve more than one goal. Indeed, more than one reason may be necessary because, in law, an intention to achieve some purpose often precludes that purpose. For example, the

Income Tax Act in broad terms forbids someone from arranging their affairs with the intention of avoiding tax. Therefore, this could never be the sole purpose for establishing a trust.

There are also several pieces of law that void (or stop) transactions and arrangements where the intention is to defeat one's creditors. Thus placing assets into a trust where the purpose is clearly (and perhaps solely) to avoid paying a creditor means the arrangement can be set aside and the transaction reversed. Thus, you may have got all of your assets out of your name and into the trust's name; however, if your intention at the time of doing this was to defeat your creditors, the trust arrangement could be overturned.

In most cases the aim is for the individual to own less, which, on the surface, seems strange. Surely the purpose of working (some would say the purpose of being alive) is to accumulate assets, not to get rid of them? Why would people want to divest themselves of hard-earned assets? Broadly, there are four reasons: taxation, asset and means testing, asset protection, and an individual's personal and family situation.

TAXATION

The days when trusts enjoyed a lower, concessional rate of tax are, regrettably, gone. For many years trusts were taxed at a rate of 10 per cent lower than companies, and up until about 25 years ago this was one of the major reasons why people put income-earning assets into trusts. However, trusts are now taxed at a higher rate than companies (28 cents for companies, 33 cents for trusts), and so that reason for trusts is gone. Nevertheless, because of the way that beneficiary income is taxed, trusts can still bring some taxation benefits to a small group of people — it is possible to distribute income to lower-income members of the family (this is called income splitting) and so some people can make tax savings (see Income Tax below).

The top personal tax rate in New Zealand changed from 1 October 2010. In fact, tax rates changed across the board at that time: the bottom rate of tax is 10.5 per cent on the first $14,000 p.a., then 17.5 per cent for income from $14,001 p.a. to $48,000 p.a., 30 per cent on income from $48,001 to $70,000 p.a., and 33 per cent on all income above $70,000 p.a. Family trusts are taxed at a flat rate of 33 per cent, and companies at a flat rate of 28 per cent.

Because of the different personal rates of tax for different bands of income, there is a substantial advantage for people who can split income among family members, and for those who trade their businesses or own investments in a company. Trusts can also give advantages for tax purposes, as income can be split among family members to make the most of the lower tax rates. However, tax rates change frequently, and you should therefore check with an accountant before making any decisions.

INCOME TAX

Trusts are a very good means of effecting income splitting (or the division of taxable income between several individuals, thus allowing lower tax rates). If income-earning assets (such as rental property, a business and interest-earning deposits) are placed in trusts, the income from those assets can be channelled off to beneficiaries. In many cases the beneficiaries will be children who have no other income. Provided the beneficiary is not a minor (under 16 years), he or she will pay tax at the rate of 10.5 per cent up to $14,000 p.a., rather than the rate of 30 per cent for income above $48,000 p.a., or 33 per cent for income above $70,000 p.a.

This allows a family with a relatively high income to split its income among all family members. Let's look at an example:

A family of five (husband, wife and three children) has a business producing a total taxable income of $190,000. If one spouse, say the husband, owned the whole business, he would pay tax on all of the income above $70,000 at the rate of 33 per cent, a total of $53,620.

However, if the business were owned by a trust, the trust could have the option of paying the income out to all of the beneficiaries in the most tax-efficient way. If all five members of the family were beneficiaries, as is most likely, each could receive income of $38,000, which would be taxed at the lower rates up to 17.5 per cent.

With each family member paying $5670 in tax, the total tax paid would be $28,350. If we compare this to the tax that would have been paid if all of the income came into just one person's hands, the saving would be $25,270 each year.

This tax saving of over $25,000 each year comes about because splitting income means that each family member is on the lower rates of tax. Having just one person with all the income would mean that the highest tax rates are paid, resulting in a much higher tax bill.

You do not need to justify distributing income to a beneficiary. This is one area where trusts differ from companies. With companies, any money paid out to family must be justified by that family member's personal exertion — i.e. they must have worked for it. There is no such problem with trusts: the trustees have the discretion to make income distributions to beneficiaries whenever they choose.

Here is another example of how income splitting can help in a family situation:

> *Both the husband and the wife work, and each has a salary of $70,000. In addition to their salaries they have an income of $20,000 from a rental property. Normally this income would be added to their salaries and, because of their other income, would be taxed at 33 per cent.*
>
> *However, if the rental property were placed in a trust the income could be credited to the couple's children. Provided those children had little or no income and were not minors, this would be taxed at 10.5 per cent. They would be saving the difference between paying tax at 33 per cent and 10.5 per cent.*

Income splitting from a family trust to minors (under 16 years) means that they will no longer be taxed at their own rate but, instead, at 33 cents in the dollar. For many people, this will remove one of the taxation advantages of trusts. Beneficiaries of trusts who are 16 years of age or older will continue to be taxed at their own personal tax rates.

The above examples assume that the children are not minors and that the parents can afford to distribute to the children. At age 18, the money becomes the children's and they can do what they like with it. Few families operate like this, although there are some who, in the past, have established trusts for this purpose.

It may be that further tax savings can be made by the use of a company. Remember that the top marginal personal tax rate is 33 per cent and the trust tax rate is a flat 33 per cent, while companies are currently taxed at 28 per cent. To avoid anyone ever paying a tax rate of more than 28 per cent, it may be a good idea to have assets owned by a company, the shares of which are owned by a trust. Some of these kinds of arrangements are frequently used; however, they have recently been targeted by the IRD as tax avoidance, and so you need very good advice before going down this route.

The income-splitting tax advantages of a family trust in many instances could easily become a target of the anti-tax-avoidance sections of the Income Tax Act, as mentioned earlier. Such arrangements could thereby be prohibited if tax avoidance were their only purpose or intent. The IRD has the power to overturn such arrangements and assess tax as if the arrangements had never taken place.

Therefore, you always need other stated reasons for arranging your affairs in such a way. With family trusts this is not difficult. The other reasons ought to be recorded at the time of establishing the trust, so that any investigation or audit in the future does not create difficulties.

USE OF ANOTHER ENTITY

Often taxpayers (particularly business people and investors) need a separate entity through which to conduct their business or investment. Sometimes it is not enough to form another company (with you as principal or controlling the shareholding) because it is not sufficiently separate.

A trust can be that separate entity, particularly if you are not a trustee or beneficiary. There are several instances where this can be important for the minimisation of tax.

The first concerns people who have been trading in shares. Such people will have been deemed a trader by the IRD and will pay tax on any profits from their share trading. This means that even shares bought as a long-term investment (rather than for short-term trading) may be defined as part of the taxpayer's share-trading activities. Once an individual is deemed by the IRD to be a share trader, most if not all of their share sale and purchase activities will be taxable.

A trust can provide another entity in which you can hold shares that you have bought for long-term investment. They will not therefore be caught up in your share-trading business, and because the trust has purchased them for long-term investment, tax will not be paid on any capital profits.

Property developers face a similar problem. Once individuals have been deemed by the IRD to be property developers they will pay tax on the profits from the sale of virtually any land, even if they had bought it for long-term investment with no intention of developing it. The exceptions are their private residence, business premises or land they have held for at least 10 years.

The tax problems associated with being deemed a developer do not simply rest with the individual — there is also a tainting of any companies in which the developer or his or her spouse and infant children have a greater than 25 per cent shareholding. A property developer will therefore have difficulty in maintaining a property-investment portfolio.

In the past, many property developers used trusts as entities to hold properties they regarded as investments rather than as development opportunities. This was because of the rules that effectively require property developers to pay tax on profits from all property sales (other than the family home and business premises). Developers found that any company of which they were a 25 per cent or greater shareholder was also 'tainted' and they needed to pay tax on capital profits.

ASSET AND MEANS TESTING

There has been much publicity over the years about asset testing, centring particularly on the outcry from older people against the much-publicised asset-testing regime for rest-home subsidies.

People will always try to avoid laws that they perceive to

be unfair. So it is with asset testing — many people have put arrangements in place, particularly using family trusts, to get around the rules and so continue to get subsidies for rest-home care.

Access to rest-home subsidies is asset-tested. For married or de facto couples, two different asset thresholds have been applied since 2011:

— a maximum of $210,000 including the family home and car (Option A); or

— a maximum of $115,000 excluding the family home and car (Option B).

A couple is able to choose which asset threshold they wish to apply under. Single people are only able to apply under Option A. In 2020, the assets allowable have been adjusted to $230,495 (Option A) or $126,224 (Option B).

The effect is that a person is expected to use the proceeds from their assets before they can get any subsidy from the government for the costs of going into a rest home. Very often the family home needs to be sold and other assets cashed up, even motor vehicles and expensive pieces of furniture and art. And rest-home care is expensive — usually about $50,000 a year. At that rate an asset base is quickly used up.

People of more modest means are often most badly affected. Someone whose only real asset is their house, valued at say $600,000, sees the equity in their only major investment

PROPERTY DEVELOPERS

There have long been rules to cover property developers (who ought to pay tax on the profits on the sale of property) who try to treat their developments as investments (and therefore not pay tax). With a smart accountant and lawyer, these rules were fairly easy to circumvent (generally with the use of a trust). In 2009, these rules were tightened considerably so that developers were stopped from running two businesses — one for their developments and one for their investments.

Now it is virtually impossible for property developers to do this: if you develop property, then any entity (trust, company, partnership, etc.) that is associated with you is also a developer and so must pay tax on the capital gains of any property.

The rules are quite comprehensive (smart lawyers and accountants, or not), and, if you are a developer or associated with a developer, the only properties where capital gains will not be paid are your own home or business premises.

dissipated within three or four years of going into a rest home. They watch their capital being steadily eroded while they may still have a number of years to live.

When their assets have been reduced below the appropriate threshold, they can get a subsidy for their continuing rest-home care. At this point they will no longer receive their New Zealand Superannuation — just a small amount for 'pocket money'.

This is quite a common scenario. Being left with virtually nothing after years of hard work creates feelings of anger and bitterness. Many find there is nothing left to pass on to children and grandchildren. It is little wonder that many people cast around for a means of avoiding what they see as a very harsh and unfair system.

LIVING WILLS

Establishing a family trust can be a solution. By placing your assets in trust for your children and grandchildren at an early stage you can receive a rest-home subsidy while knowing that your assets are securely held — initially for your own benefit if you do happen to need anything, and subsequently for your family.

Family trusts are sometimes called 'living wills', as in effect they bring forward the passing on of assets. Setting up such a trust as a means of avoiding asset testing can be a simple matter when relatively small assets, such as the family home, are placed in trust. Such a trust is often most beneficial for those with modest estates.

People with large amounts of assets may have little interest in avoiding asset testing. Their wealth is such that if they have to spend a few years in a rest home the payment for their care will not make a significant dent in their net worth.

When being assessed for a rest-home subsidy, the MSD will look at any gifts that you have made in the past. If there is gifting:

— over $6000 in any year in the previous five years, or

— over $27,000 in any other year,

you could be declined a subsidy. With the repeal of gift duties, the MSD looks even more closely at any gifts that have been made. The MSD has the ability to decline a subsidy where an individual has deprived themselves of an asset, and will certainly look hard at major amounts of gifting when considering a rest-home subsidy.

There are now few people who can successfully use a family trust to defeat the asset-testing regime. Gifting is carefully scrutinised by the MSD, and if there is gifting over $27,000 in any one year the application for a subsidy will likely be declined. Note that this $27,000 p.a. is for a couple or a single person; the amount is the same.

This more strict scrutiny of gifting has come at a time when people have more valuable assets. House values, in particular, have grown, and this means that, with a threshold of $27,000 p.a. for a couple, gifting a house is more difficult over any reasonable timeframe.

ASSET PROTECTION

It is now very common for business and professional people to have a family trust holding some of their assets. Protection from creditors has been a primary purpose of trusts for a very long time. The protection can extend much further than creditors, too; sometimes to a disgruntled ex-spouse or ex-partner.

Asset protection is one of the most difficult outcomes to achieve, and great care is required in structuring a trust and putting the arrangements in place.

Typically, when we talk of the need for asset protection and protection from creditors, we immediately think of the time after the 2008 Global Financial Crisis when there were many bankruptcies, some of them very high-profile (and some of whom were going bankrupt for the second time). Yet the conspicuous consumption of these people carried on just as before. This irritated many people — not only their creditors, but also the general public.

Business is cyclical — there are always ups and downs. The risks of business are such that many people take the opportunity in good times to tuck away some of their assets in a trust for safekeeping. These assets are then unavailable to creditors in the event of business difficulties or failure.

Sizeable funds can be built up in trusts, which are quarantined from the rest of the person's business affairs. Indeed some family trusts hold the majority of a person's assets, trading and carrying out business in their own right. Yet these assets cannot be touched in the event that the settlor is bankrupted.

Of course, there is often litigation regarding assets that are held in trust. Creditors (or the Official Assignee) may try to overturn a trust arrangement and successfully argue that the trust is a sham. This would make the assets in the trust available to creditors.

While there has been considerable public distaste for business people who have used trusts to avoid their creditors, in my experience assets held in trust become a bargaining point in the event of insolvency. Sometimes what happens is that a deal is made. Creditors (be they banks or trade creditors) are offered funds out of the trust that they might not get in a bankruptcy situation, providing they agree not to pursue the person to bankruptcy. This is far more common than a debtor simply allowing him- or herself to go into bankruptcy while a trust continues to hold assets.

Some people argue that there is little point in using a trust for asset-protection purposes because the bank will often require a personal guarantee as well as a guarantee from the trust (often supported by a mortgage over the trust's property). This is usually true — it is very difficult to protect yourself from the bank with its demands for security and guarantees from all entities, including the family trust. However, other creditors (e.g. trade creditors and sometimes the IRD) can be protected against by a family trust.

PROTECTION FOR PROFESSIONAL PEOPLE

Professional people (especially lawyers and accountants) often use trusts to protect themselves from financial difficulties. They are in business like anyone else and subject to business failure. In addition there may be claims against them for negligence and malpractice, and they could be left vulnerable as a result of the actions of their partners. All of this conspires to place professionals particularly at risk. The widespread use of trusts among professionals is a reflection of that risk.

CREDITORS' RIGHTS

The creation of a family trust and the disposal of assets into it is no guarantee of protection against one's creditors. Creditors have means at their disposal to attack any arrangement by which people have disposed of assets to a creditor's disadvantage. These approaches derive from two pieces of law: the Insolvency Act 2006 and the Property Law Act 2007.

The Insolvency Act 2006

The Official Assignee can void (that is, set aside) any gift made within two years of the donor being adjudicated bankrupt. Therefore any family trust arrangement would have to see all gifting completed two years before the settlor had gone bankrupt. Otherwise any gifts made within that two-year period can be claimed back from the recipient. In the case of a family trust, this means the Official Assignee would approach the trust and request that it give back the gifts it had received.

There is a further difficulty with the Insolvency Act arising from section 205, which allows the Official Assignee to set aside any gifts made within five years of the bankruptcy if the donor was insolvent at the time of making the gift. While solvency can be difficult to prove either way (particularly five years previously), section 205 of the Insolvency Act certainly requires thought and care.

It would be advisable to complete a 'solvency certificate' recording your financial position when making any large gifts, and to obtain independent certification from your accountant as to your financial position.

The Property Law Act 2007

Sections 344 to 350 deal mostly with people's intentions when they dispose of property; alienation of assets with an intent to defraud creditors can be voided. The important thing here is a person's intention at the time they disposed of assets. If they had clearly got rid of assets solely to defeat creditors and avoid paying debts, such transactions can be set aside and declared void.

Historically, intention has been difficult to prove — particularly if the disposal of assets took place several years previously. Our intentions are personal and are often not recorded at the time. Someone looking at family trust transactions that had occurred several years earlier would find difficulty in proving that the intention was to defeat creditors. However, a Supreme Court case has changed the test for intention. It is now clear that the courts will be more willing to imply an intention to defraud creditors from circumstances, rather than requiring creditors to prove that a person acted with intent to defraud. For example, the disposal of an asset by an insolvent person to a trust is likely to be considered an intent to defraud.

This approach to intent to defraud opens up more opportunities for creditors to attack the disposal of assets to a trust. Accordingly, care needs to be taken when transferring assets to a trust if this will impact on existing creditors.

The implications of the Insolvency Act and the Property Law Act mean it is better to establish a family trust sooner rather than later. The repeal of gift duties means that those in business or a profession should mostly act very quickly to get assets out of their own name and into a trust. The passage of time blurs purpose, intent and solvency, and makes your family trust arrangement much less susceptible to a successful attack from creditors. The time to put assets away into a trust is when things are going well, not just before a business failure.

Trusts have been used for centuries to keep assets away from creditors of various types. Your trust arrangements may not always guarantee asset protection, but they will at the very least make it more difficult for creditors to get at your assets — and provide you with a strong bargaining position.

THE MORALITY OF ASSET PROTECTION THROUGH TRUSTS

The issue of morality weighs heavily on the minds of many people with regard to the use of trusts for asset protection.

Many people see trusts as a way of helping people escape their rightful obligations.

There have been several well-publicised instances of high-profile businessmen (and they *are* all men) who have gone bankrupt (and even to jail) but still carried on the same lifestyle afterwards. A story in Australia has it that one particularly well-known businessman came off the rich list upon going bankrupt, only to be replaced immediately by his wife. There is considerable public distaste for this behaviour, and a widely held belief that such people should fulfil their obligations and pay their dues.

At the other end of the spectrum the legitimate use of trusts for asset-protection purposes would, I believe, be accepted and approved of by the vast majority of people. A good example of this is a case I was once involved with. This family consisted of a panelbeater and his wife (both in their early forties) and their two teenage children. The panelbeater had worked all his life as a wage and salary earner, and the family had just paid off the mortgage. The children were soon to leave home. The couple started to believe that life might in fact have begun at 40.

The problem was that the panelbeater wanted to fulfil a lifetime dream of setting up his own business. His wife, however, believed that with the family situation now secure they could look forward to another 40 or 50 years of life in peace (without the children) and security (without the mortgage).

Each remained adamant and the dispute went on for some time, until eventually the wife agreed that her husband could go into business on his own account — with one proviso. The proviso was that the house was put away in trust for her and the children so that, regardless of how the business went, the house would remain safe for the family.

Between these two scenarios (the panelbeater and the high-profile businessman) exist a vast number of situations, and each sits somewhere on the morality spectrum. Exactly where each one sits is up to the individual to decide.

I would, however, put forward two considerations when talking about the morality of family trusts. The first is that by putting aside assets in trust you do at least have a choice as to whether or not you pay creditors who would otherwise remain unpaid. If your business failure has been caused through no fault of your own (e.g. from the economic fallout of COVID) and you have assets in trust, you may choose to pay creditors out of your trust. You can decide according to your situation and your own sense of right and wrong, but at least you have a choice.

The other point that needs to be considered is the concept of limited liability, which is in reality what we are talking about. The concept of limited liability through companies exists so that people can invest in businesses while not being personally liable. How many people would invest on the sharemarket if their personal liability were not limited? I would suggest that the vast majority of companies on the New Zealand sharemarket would simply not exist. Trusts are an extension of that concept of limited liability.

PERSONAL AND FAMILY REASONS

Families come in many shapes, sizes and situations. In the past, family trusts have been used to keep certain matters confidential; for example, people want to benefit children from previous relationships without their current family's knowledge. This happened more frequently than many would realise, and, although it may seem Victorian, I know of at least three such instances currently.

A family trust used to be a good vehicle to execute such wishes. However, with the Trusts Act it will be much harder, maybe impossible. The disclosures that will now be required for beneficiaries will make such confidentiality difficult to maintain.

Nevertheless, trusts have been, and will continue to be, used to resolve family issues.

CONTROLLING FAMILY MEMBERS

Trusts may be used to control certain family members, or to make a benefit consequent upon certain events taking place. For example, a beneficiary (perhaps one who is a child of the settlor) may only benefit from the trust provided he or she is married, or perhaps continues to manage the family business efficiently, or attains some stated qualification. While such conditions may sound somewhat harsh, they are at times the sort of things that are important within families.

The control of 'spendthrift' children is another common reason for forming a trust. A trust can allow investments to be held by a trustee, with children receiving only income from them, not capital. The investments themselves may never pass to the settlor's children, but may skip a generation to the grandchildren. This can protect the capital from children suspected of irresponsibility, or reflect the settlor's belief that children should make their own way in the world. It is the same with the family business or farm. Children may be allowed to manage and derive income from the business but not actually own it. This keeps the business intact, preventing the children from breaking it up or selling it to get capital.

It also provides checks and balances for major acquisitions or disposals within the business. Major moves would require the trustees' approval and compliance, which would be given only with good reason.

SUCCESSION

Trusts can be very good vehicles for succession, especially when children are young. If we consider simultaneous death a possibility (and we should: car crash, house fire, boating accident, etc.), the discretionary nature of a family trust allows for the people's wills to put all assets into a family trust and good (i.e. trustworthy) new trustees to be appointed to continue the trust and make distributions as and when they seem best for the children. This means that children do not receive funds on attaining a certain arbitrary age as they usually do with a will. The new trustees are guided by a memorandum of wishes and exercise their judgement accordingly.

SUMMARY

The formation of a family trust is particular and specific to each individual. While the reasons for establishing a trust have been broadly categorised in this book, each person settling a trust will have their own particular (and probably quite personal) reasons.

No other vehicle for ownership has the same flexibility as a family trust. The settlor no longer owns the assets but continues to have the use and benefit of them, as well as some control over them. The assets do not appear on any statement of position (perhaps for a creditor, bank or government agency) but, although you are no longer the registered owner of, say, your family home, you will probably carry on living there just as you always have.

If your advisers do not know you and your family well, spend some time with them so that they get to know your position, your background and what you are trying to achieve through the formation of a trust. A family trust is not like a limited liability company to be bought off the shelf with a standard constitution suitable for everyone. Regrettably, I have too often seen advisers doing family trust work as if everybody were the same. Each trust should be tailored to the individual's requirements.

BE VERY CLEAR ABOUT WHAT YOU WANT

There are many decisions to be made: who the trustees are, who the beneficiaries are, whether or not assets are gifted to the trust or left as a debt owing back to you, what assets are to be sold to the trust, whether the debt back to you will be upon demand or be entrenched for a period, and so on. These decisions can be made intelligently only if you are clear about what you want to achieve. You may need to prioritise your aims.

In structuring your trust you may find some objectives will preclude others. For example, if you are concerned by the possibility of a reintroduction of estate duties, and the avoidance of such a tax is a primary aim for your trust, you cannot structure the arrangement so that you are both settlor and beneficiary, as this was specifically excluded in the legislation of the time and probably would be again if these taxes returned. How, then, do you obtain income or capital from the trust?

These seemingly conflicting requirements demand some thought. A solution might be to place only some assets in the trust, leaving out others (which are perhaps income-producing) on which you can live. A second possible solution is to have a second trust (there is no reason why not) with different beneficiaries (one of whom would be you) and its own share of your assets. Still another solution would be to ensure that there is a substantial debt owed back to you that would not be gifted immediately, but would be available for you to draw on to meet your living requirements.

Get good advice, and be very clear about why you are doing what you are doing.

Q If I only put the family home into the trust, how can I get cash out of it?

A Only by selling the house or by mortgaging it. Generally, most people put their house in a trust to protect it in some way — perhaps because they are going into business or for asset-testing purposes. Drawing out cash is not one of the aims — the family home will not generate cash, regardless of who the owner is. A family trust in itself cannot turn one dollar into two.

You can only draw cash in the same way as if you owned the assets yourself. Of course if the assets are income-producing investments, you may draw out that income if you need it, either by being a beneficiary or drawing on the debt that the trust owes you. But if the assets are not income-producing (such as the family home, holiday home, art, antiques, etc.), a family trust does not give any advantage in terms of access to cash.

4

Relationships and Trusts

F amily trusts have always been an important vehicle for arranging affairs in terms of relationships with others. One good reason for their usefulness is the changing nature of relationships themselves. Marriage is no longer necessarily for life: separation is very common and can happen to anyone. Other domestic arrangements, such as civil unions, de facto marriages and same-sex marriages, are increasingly common, as are blended families. The Property (Relationships) Act 1976 covers all of these arrangements.

A second factor to come into consideration is the Property (Relationships) Act itself, a piece of legislation that radically changed the law around relationship property and its sharing. The implications of this social and legal climate are that you should be prepared to give careful consideration to the way you plan to preserve and eventually dispose of your assets.

THE PROPERTY (RELATIONSHIPS) ACT 1976

The main points of the Act are:

— The Act applies to married couples, civil unions and those living in de facto relationships (including same-sex couples). It could even apply to siblings or friends living together, sexual relations not being an absolutely essential part of the definition of a relationship.

— The relationship must have lasted for at least three years for the property-sharing provisions to apply. There are exceptions to this, though; particularly if there has been a child of the relationship.

— Living together as a couple has been defined in terms of such things as the extent to which the couple share a home, do household chores, have a mutual commitment to a shared life, and how they hold themselves out to family and friends, whether there is a sexual relationship, and the care and support of any children. Courts may attach weight to each of these as is appropriate in each case, and no one factor is essential for a relationship to exist and for the Act to apply.

— Property is divided between relationship property and separate property.

— Relationship property will be shared on the break-up of the relationship. Relationship property is property that is intended for the common use or benefit of the couple, and includes such things as the family home and family chattels (furniture, car or boat) and the value of superannuation schemes that were paid into during the relationship.

— Separate property is everything else and will not be divided, provided that it was not for common use and benefit.

— Debts (including student loans) are shared in the same way as assets. Whether a debt is classified as relationship debt (and therefore shared) or separate will depend on what the loan has been used for.

— The court may award one partner a greater share of the couple's property if the earning capacity of one partner is likely to be greater because of the contributions of his or her partner. For example, if one partner had stayed at home to look after the children while the other continued to develop a career, the partner who stayed at home could be awarded more of the assets.

— There are contracting-out provisions, which must be in writing and each partner must have been advised by a lawyer before signing.

— Courts may set aside asset transfers to trusts that were entered into during a relationship where there was the intention to defeat the rights of one of the partners, or where the transfer of property to a trust had the effect of defeating the other's rights.

— The Act covers the division of property if one partner dies. The surviving partner will be able to choose whether to take what was left in the will or may make a claim to receive their entitlement of the couple's relationship property.

The Act addresses the changes in society outlined above, and does bring certain benefits. Some of them are:

— This area of law was previously very uncertain and could involve very expensive litigation. The Act brings greater certainty regarding the rights of people in what may be perceived as an unconventional relationship (although there is of course still a considerable amount of litigation).

— It supports a valid contracting out or a prenuptial agreement previously entered into by a couple.

— It protects the rights of a partner in a relationship to property that has been previously transferred into a trust. The following scenario is rare, but not unknown. One of the partners (say, the husband) has driven the formation of the trust (perhaps for asset-protection purposes) and appointed as trustees his accountant and lawyer. When the marriage fails the husband effectively controls the trust and the wife has little influence to win back what were previously her assets. The Act ensures that her rights to property are not adversely affected by the couple's setting up of the trust.

IMPLICATIONS OF THE ACT

The passing of the Act widened the implications of property sharing on relationship failure, because rules that were previously only relevant to legal marriages were now applied to those living in de facto relationships.

There are currently nearly 250,000 people in New Zealand living in heterosexual de facto relationships, with many more in same-sex de facto relationships: and the Act means they have the same property rights as a married couple. For example, if a couple were living in a home belonging to one of the partners, the other partner would previously have had limited grounds to make any claim on that house. When the Act was amended in 2002, that home became relationship property and would be divided if the relationship failed. The Act therefore had the effect of giving a right to a share in property that the other partner previously did not have. (However, room for vigorous argument remains, particularly regarding whether the partners were indeed living as a couple, and when they started living as a couple.)

Some of these relationships will be long-standing relationships that do not effectively differ from a marriage. Others may be less committed, a more casual type of live-in relationship. Both are caught by the Act, and so especially where there are substantial assets involved some action needs to be taken. This means that people in less formal relationships may have to think about their relationship-property ownership. Those who are currently in a de facto relationship (particularly one that is getting close to the three-year mark) need to take advice and discuss with their partners how they would want their assets to be divided if the relationship fails. This conversation is not always easy, but nevertheless where there are substantial assets — or the prospect of substantial assets at some time in the future (perhaps through an inheritance) — it needs to be done. Hard though it may be to broach the subject, it seems better to arrange things fairly while you are still in love, rather than at the end of the relationship when things are much more difficult. For many, the simplest way is to contract out with a property-sharing agreement that is properly entered into.

The Property (Relationships) Act was last changed nearly 20 years ago (in 2002). In 2018, the Law Commission proposed further changes to the Act to reflect social change. Proposed changes included that the family home would no longer be shared equally, and that assets held in trust would not be excluded from the pool for division. This is, of course, a long way from becoming law, but it is nevertheless likely that there will be ongoing change in this area.

CONTRACTING OUT

As outlined earlier, it is possible to contract out of the Act, with each partner agreeing that he or she will take certain assets if the relationship fails. This contracting out can take place either before the relationship is entered into or during it. Providing that these agreements have been properly entered into — the agreement must be in writing, and each partner must have been advised by a lawyer before signing the agreement — it will be harder to have them overturned than it used to be. A court can only set aside an agreement if it thinks that serious injustice would result if it let the agreement stand.

RELATIONSHIP PROPERTY AND TRUSTS

Trusts have long been used by people to solve property issues in marriage and relationships. The general principle has been that, because assets that are owned in a trust are not personally owned, they do not form part of matrimonial or relationship property, and therefore are not divided when a marriage or relationship fails. People with substantial assets could therefore put assets into a trust before a marriage so that they would not lose them (or at least a part of them) if the marriage later broke up. Older people, and those going into second or subsequent marriages and relationships, are often most affected by this, because they frequently come into the marriage or relationship with unequal amounts of assets, one of the partners could be quite vulnerable, and there might well be a number of children of different parentage involved.

Trusts can be a part of the arrangement that people might think about to make sure that assets stay where their owner intends. There are a number of different circumstances where a trust should be considered.

SINGLE PEOPLE

Many young people go into a relationship without a thought that it might end one day. They may own very little, and so splitting up is not a great property issue — although the creeping accumulation of assets happens to nearly everyone, and there have been many bitter arguments about who gets the tablet or the bed.

However, single people who have significant assets, especially those who have just come out of a relationship, should think about putting their assets in a trust. People coming out of a relationship are sometimes not particularly open to suggestions about preparing for another relationship, but it is when you are single that you should plan. Separation is a time when you will be rearranging your finances anyway — so it's a good time to consider the possibility of a trust.

The key thing is to transfer assets that could in the future become relationship property, especially your home. Remember that, if a new partner moves into your home, that person could well be able to make a claim on it when he or she moves out. It is quite true that you will be able to contract out of the Property (Relationships) Act 1976; however, if you have transferred assets to a trust, your assets may avoid ever becoming an issue within a new relationship. In this respect, family trusts have been called the 'coward's prenuptial agreement'. With assets in a trust, you may never need even to talk about a prenuptial agreement.

Having said this, care is needed in structuring trusts, because trusts can be overturned by a court (see page 95).

PEOPLE IN RELATIONSHIPS AND MARRIAGES

The effect of the Act is that people in qualifying de facto relationships have the same property rights as married couples and those in civil unions. For example, if your partner has been living in 'your' home for over three years and you have no agreement to the contrary, he or she will probably have a right to half of your home. At that point, your partner can refuse to opt out of the Act — you cannot force him or her to sign a contract stating otherwise.

Nor would you be able simply to set up a trust for your home. As mentioned earlier, a trust that defeats one partner's rights to property is able to be set aside more easily. This ought to have the beneficial effect of ensuring that, at the time a trust is formed, both partners are well advised of what is happening and both partners make sure that they are trustees or have someone as trustee who is sympathetic to them.

Those who are in relationships and who are contemplating a trust for their assets should take action as soon as possible. If your partner has a right to the property due to your relationship, he or she will have to be consulted and should approve the transfer to the trust if it is to stand up to scrutiny later. Ideally, a contracting-out agreement would be entered into in conjunction with the establishment of the trust.

SEPARATING COUPLES

Trusts no doubt will continue to be used by couples who are separating to help share their property fairly. For example, a separating couple might agree that he will take the business while she will keep the family home. However, the holiday house is still in dispute. A solution might be to put the holiday home in trust for the whole family so that even after the separation all members can use it.

A more emotional issue is that many people who separate want to make sure that what were once their assets will go to the children of the couple — not to a new partner or the children of the new partner or even other children that their ex-partner might have. It is quite common for one partner to feel quite strongly that only the children of the relationship should benefit from assets that were obtained through that relationship. A trust can do this, because the beneficiaries can be specifically named, thereby excluding further children from other relationships.

Although trusts, as already mentioned, have been called the 'coward's prenuptial agreement', you should not think that putting your assets in a trust means that you are completely protected from a partner. A trust may help to keep personal property separate; however, there have been many successful instances in which trusts have been attacked. In setting up a trust for this purpose you should be sure to get good advice from a specialist family law expert, and not rely solely on the use of a family trust.

PARENTS AND SUCCESSION

Most of us become parents at some stage. Yet we are a group of people who have often not thought through the implications of relationship property regarding our children. But we need to if we want our assets to stay in the family or go where we intend. We need to formulate a plan that will enable us to achieve our goals.

Most people have a will that names their children (or sometimes grandchildren) as beneficiaries. However, what a lot of people do not realise is that if their children receive an inheritance, the spouses or partners of their children may end up with a part of the inheritance.

A common scenario: a daughter receives an inheritance from her parents. She uses this money to buy a house for herself and her partner, or uses it to repay the mortgage, or to buy some other asset that is for the joint benefit of the couple. If her marriage or relationship should fail at some time in the future, her husband would have a claim on the inheritance or what it was invested in.

Parents need to think hard about whether they would be comfortable for their assets to go to their son-in-law or daughter-in-law. You may like your child's spouse and believe that their relationship is stable. However, you do need to ask yourself how comfortable you would be to know that your assets were going outside of your immediate family.

A story that I heard years ago illustrates this point very well:

A farmer had just one daughter, and he wanted to pass on the farm to her. The daughter was keen to take over the farm; however, she had demonstrated what her father considered to be very poor judgement in marrying 'a good-for-nothing lazy layabout' — the farmer was not at all keen on his son-in-law. What's more, he knew that if he passed the farm on to his daughter and the marriage failed, the son-in-law could end up with half of the farm. So instead of passing the farm on to his daughter under his will, the farmer put the farm into a family trust. His daughter and her husband farmed the property almost as if it were their own — but if the marriage should fail, the farm would not be the property of the daughter and so not be available for division.

Parents and grandparents need to think very hard about how they are going to pass on their assets to their children. Such thinking became even more compelling with the passage of the Property (Relationships) Act 1976. It may be that you are comfortable enough with seeing your children share their inheritances (which have come from you) with their spouses, particularly if they are in marriages of long standing and there are children from the marriage. However, your children may have relatively casual live-in relationships, even when they are quite young.

Remember that if the live-in relationship lasts three years, and assets have been intermingled and used for joint benefit,

CHILDREN'S TRUSTS

Some people do not have their children as beneficiaries of their wills, but instead have the children's own trusts as beneficiaries. This was sometimes done to avoid the gifting process — instead of the assets going to the children and then spending years and decades gifting, it was easier to simply have the assets go straight to the trust. With the repeal of gift duty, this reason for having children's trusts as beneficiaries is less necessary.

The other reason for assets to go to a child's trust rather than to the child personally could be to avoid assets being intermingled with those of the child's partner and so becoming relationship property. If assets go directly to the child, there is a strong chance that they become relationship property, whereas the trust fund can be kept separate. Some parents go an extra step by forming trusts for each of their children (assuming they have not already formed one). The trusts sit with no assets until the parents' deaths.

the assets will probably be divided equally. What you may see as just a passing infatuation (albeit a live-in one) could in fact have much more serious implications — for you and your succession planning.

You do not have to be too imaginative to create the following scenario:

> *Jay and Carole leave school at age 18 and go to university. They go flatting together in a group flat. A relationship develops and the two move into the same room (no doubt they will tell you that it is to save money). In their third year at university, Jay's parents are killed in a car crash. Jay is left an inheritance of $520,000, and he uses the money to buy a small house. Carole and he move into it, along with some other people who rent the spare rooms. Three years later Carole leaves — and makes a claim for her half of the house. She would probably win that claim — and so half of the inheritance that had come from Jay's parents would go to Carole, something that they would never have wanted.*

There are three things that can be done to avoid a situation like this:

1. You could try to educate your children not to intermingle any inheritance from you. This might work — but it might not. If it seems like a good idea to buy a house or to pay off

the mortgage with an inheritance, that is what is likely to happen regardless of all of your warnings.

2. You could write your will so that on your death a testamentary trust is formed — a trust formed under terms spelled out in your will. It would see assets stay in trust for a period that is set out in your will or until some stipulated occurrence happens (e.g. grandchildren are born). This works perfectly well and is a very real option for a lot of people. The only downside is that you never see the trust work (it only comes into being after you are dead) and you have to hope that the terms of it are correctly set. There is no flexibility, little discretion for the trustees, and no ability to change the terms of the trust if events make that desirable.

3. You could form a family trust now for your assets and set out in your memorandum of wishes what you want to happen to the trust and its assets after you have gone. This may be for assets to stay in the trust so that your children have the use or benefit of the assets but not ownership of them. The example of the farmer illustrates this scenario well. If your children need money from the trust, the trust can lend it to them. For example, if after you have died the trust cashes up its investments and property, and your children would like to pay off their mortgages, the trust could *lend* them the money to do so. In that way, if their relationships or marriages fail, the money from the trust

that went to repay the joint mortgage is not lost to your own child, as it is a debt that the couple needs to repay to the trust.

One of the big advantages of using family trusts for this is the flexibility that they offer and the high level of discretion of the trustees. The trustees are not bound to make distributions because of stipulated events but can use their judgement. This is a double-edged sword of course: they need to use their discretion wisely, and to think about what you would have wanted. As always, you want to appoint good trustees and instruct them well on what it is that you are trying to achieve.

Q I am a beneficiary of the trust that I have settled. Can the potential benefit that I might receive be an asset to be shared under the Property (Relationships) Act 1976?

A No, not if the trust is a discretionary one (which most family trusts are). If the trust is discretionary, you have no absolute right to any benefits in the future. (You may benefit or you may not, and that decision is up to the trustees.) The situation can be different in the case of a fixed trust, but it would be very unusual to have a discretionary benefit brought into a relationship as property to be shared.

5

Disadvantages of Family Trusts

There are many compelling reasons for establishing a family trust as set out in the previous two chapters. But there must be some disadvantages, otherwise everybody would have formed one. So what are the disadvantages?

For a few people there are no benefits (or at least no perceived benefits). Some do not want (or are unable) to minimise taxation, have no interest in protecting themselves against asset testing or protecting themselves against their creditors, and have no personal or family reasons for establishing a trust. The 'benefits' of a trust are not benefits for all people.

Family trusts are still quite popular. However, just because they are 'in' is no reason to form one. It may be good dinner-party conversation to drop a comment about 'my family trust', but that is not sufficient reason in my view.

There is a group who can see some benefits in forming a trust but who are talked out of it by their professional advisers.

Up until December 1992, many advisers encouraged people to create trusts for estate-planning purposes. When estate duties were abolished in December 1992 many advisers thought that the most compelling reason for having a trust had gone. They were wrong in this view, but, nevertheless, they very often attempted to dissuade people from establishing a trust.

One problem is that some lawyers are not experts on trusts. Many specialise in quite different areas of law (perhaps conveyancing or criminal law) and have not studied the subject of trusts in much detail. So for some people the greatest impediment to establishing a trust is convincing a solicitor (or other adviser) that it's a good idea.

Having said all this, it should be stated that there are drawbacks to having a trust, even if in most instances these can be overcome in one way or another. It is important that you balance the advantages with the disadvantages; look at the pros and cons. This needs to be done with the help of a skilled professional.

The disadvantages fall into three main categories: reliance on trustees, cost, and inconvenience.

RELIANCE ON TRUSTEES

When you establish a trust and sell assets into it, in nearly every respect you are alienated from those assets that are no longer in your name.

This means that you must rely on the trustees. Even if you are one of the trustees, perhaps effectively with the right of veto (quite a common form of control over a trust), you will nevertheless require the agreement and goodwill of the other trustees to achieve what you want.

Although you may put in place a range of control devices when you establish a trust, the assets are in the trustees' names and they must deal with them in compliance with the trust deed. The concept of no longer owning assets that you have worked for all your life is very frightening to many people.

Not only that, of course, but you have to rely on trustees to manage the trust well and comply with trust law, including being au fait with the provisions of the new Trusts Act.

The reliance on other people (the trustees) to own 'your' assets is where most of the horror stories regarding trustees arise. They usually concern uncooperative trustees who have little regard for the settlor's wishes.

Many of the difficulties that have befallen families with trusts have occurred with trusts that were established many years ago. Many of these older trusts had deeds that lacked the control mechanisms and the flexibility that modern trust deeds normally have. I remember one such example.

> A *family owned a business that operated out of a property owned by a trust. The trust had been established in 1962 and contained no provision for the removal of trustees. The family wished to sell the land and buildings out of the trust to one of the beneficiaries (now aged 45) as a part of a restructuring that I had recommended.*
>
> *However, although the entire family wished this*

transaction to take place, one of the trustees was unenthusiastic. This trustee was concerned that there might be beneficiaries as yet unborn who could be disadvantaged. This seemed somewhat unlikely as the only people capable of producing more beneficiaries were in their mid- to late forties, but the trustee concerned insisted on a new valuation.

On receipt of that valuation he still procrastinated, at one stage talking of approaching the High Court for guidance. This went on for some months while reports were written and family meetings held. The delay was most disadvantageous to the proposed restructuring, and only after considerable time and effort had been expended did the trustee eventually agree to the proposal.

Such a situation would be rare if a modern trust deed were in place, but this 60-year-old deed contained no clause allowing the removal of trustees. (The trustee concerned was legally and technically correct in considering the possibility that there might be beneficiaries as yet unborn. However, his reluctance to agree to a fairly common-sense proposal on the basis of a technicality cost the family both time and money.)

This example shows the importance of keeping control over trustees in some way or other. There are many forms this control can take, as outlined in Chapter 1, but in the above example the simplest way would have been the ability of the settlor to remove the trustee and appoint another.

COST

Another drawback is the cost involved in the establishment and administration of trusts.

ESTABLISHMENT COST

Having a suitable deed drawn up and executed is likely to cost between $3000 and $5000. A parallel trust arrangement (more on this later) would probably cost a little more. This cost is simply for the establishment of the trust, to get it to a position where it is ready to purchase assets.

If your bill from your solicitor (or other adviser) is more than $3500, perhaps it is because you have done something complicated, or you have changed your mind after the preliminary discussions. Most advisers charge on an hourly basis, from $300 to $500 per hour.

Another reason why your set-up cost may be more than $3500 (assuming that it is a relatively straightforward arrangement) is if your adviser is not particularly knowledgeable about trusts and has had to spend time researching the area. This shows the importance of seeking an adviser who is skilled and experienced in trust work. They should need to do little (if any) research, and be able to draw up a trust deed quickly and efficiently after ascertaining basic personal information.

Just as your trust should usually cost no more than $3500, it should not cost less than $2000. This may seem like a strange thing to say, but a trust that costs less than $2000 has either been discounted for some reason or has been produced by what I call the 'word-processor approach'. These trusts are produced by advisers who take a mass-market approach to their work, producing 'off-the-rack' trusts with little individual or personal character. Although this is less common than it once was, a trust that costs less than $2000 carries a great risk of proving unsatisfactory at some time in the future.

Be more wary of a cheap adviser than of one who is expensive. All else being equal, it is better to pay a little more and have your trust done properly. Remember that trusts are long-term vehicles and contain your most valuable assets — so you need to get it right.

A properly formed trust ought to have input from both a lawyer and an accountant (or a financial adviser). Both ought to be skilled in their work and have some knowledge of (if not specialisation in) trusts. You may find that a trust company has both legal and accounting skills and can do the entire job for you as a one-stop shop.

In addition to the cost of the trust deed, there may be other costs associated with the arrangement. This could involve conveyancing costs for property, or tax depreciation recovered for some assets. There could also be charges for ancillary documentation such as a new will or a memorandum of wishes. A reasonable all-up cost for a trust (the deed of conveyancing and other documents) could be $3000–$5000, although it could be considerably more expensive if multiple properties or other assets need to be transferred.

REGISTERING WITH THE IRD

In the event that your trust is going to have income it will

RESETTLEMENT

Most modern trust deeds have a resettlement clause in them. Resettlement is the advancement of the assets of a trust to a new trust (or trusts).

Broadly, the new trust(s) will be for the benefit of at least one of the beneficiaries of the original trust, although the terms of the new trust(s) may be somewhat different. This can allow for restructuring if the original trust arrangement has become 'inconvenient' — perhaps for a division of assets within a family or with relationship property. Note that this cannot be used to escape perpetuity rules — the original trust and the new trust(s) may not together last more than 125 years. Resettlement of trusts will be common in the near future as trustees seek to have a trust that complies with the Trusts Act in terms of default duties. For example, a trust that owns little more than the family home would put trustees in breach of their duties, as they would be seen to have not invested prudently (a prudent person would not own just one asset but would diversify). To avoid this accusation an 'eccentric' investment provision would be added to the trust deed.

You can also be a trustee yourself and require unanimous approval for any major transaction; leave some debt owing back to you that could be called up; or, perhaps most important of all, ensure that you appoint good, empathetic trustees in the first place. Do not forget that the more control you have, the greater the possibility of being caught by some future law change.

Most trustees take a far more relaxed (some would say common-sense) approach to their duties. They will go along with the settlor's wishes provided the wishes are reasonable and in accordance with the trust deed. The occasional horror stories are notable because they are exceptions to the rule.

need an IRD number. (Trusts that own only the family home and therefore have no income do not need to be registered.) Furthermore, if it is to have income above $60,000 p.a., and that income does not stem solely from investment returns or residential property, it will need a GST number.

This does not cost anything and there is nothing to stop you applying to the IRD yourself to register your trust as a trading entity and get the numbers. You will need to provide a copy of the trust deed to prove the existence of the trust, and fill out a form. From there the registration and numbers are usually quickly forthcoming.

However, you may choose to use an accountant to obtain IRD registration — they can usually do this quickly and efficiently. Of course this will mean paying for their time.

CONVEYING ASSETS TO THE TRUST

In addition to the costs of establishing the trust deed and having it registered with the IRD, there are costs in conveying some types of assets to the trust. The amount will vary depending on the type of assets and the size of the trust.

Some trusts, such as trading trusts, can require considerable input from an accountant. Mirror trusts (see Chapter 9) will always cost a little more as there are two trusts to be established, which then often form a partnership for the ownership of assets.

Interest-bearing deposits

If the trust is going to own only interest-bearing deposits, this is very straightforward. You simply approach the bank and have the deposits put in the trust's name. To do this you will probably have to produce the trust deed, but there will be no cost.

Real estate

In the case of real estate, there are almost always legal conveyancing costs, which may be quite small (in the case of the family home, probably around $1000–$2000), but could also be quite considerable. The costs involved in conveying real estate depend on the number of titles and whether they have mortgages.

Depreciation recovered may also be a problem for those with investment property and some other assets. If you have claimed depreciation and then sell your property to the trust above book value, you will have income in the form of the depreciation that you have recovered. You will need to pay tax on this income. This situation can be difficult for many people, but there may be some comfort in the knowledge that, once the assets are in the trust, the trust may be able to claim depreciation on the new, higher value.

Rental properties that have been owned for less than five years may fall foul of the 'bright line' test and have tax payable on capital gains. Given the extent of recent property booms, this could be considerable.

If you are going to transfer real estate into your trust, you should most certainly discuss the conveyancing and any other costs with your lawyer and possibly your accountant. You may also need to obtain a valuation from a real estate firm or valuer.

Shares

The transfer of shares into a trust can usually be done very cheaply, as, unlike many countries, in New Zealand there is no stamp duty on shares. Shares in publicly listed companies can be transferred by your sharebroker, who will usually do such transfers without any charge (although you should confirm this in advance). The transfer of non-listed companies is usually done quickly and efficiently by your accountant or lawyer for a very small charge.

Other assets

Assets such as unit trusts and government stock may require some input from your financial planner or the broker who arranged your purchase in the first place. In my experience such people rarely charge for such a transaction, and the managers of unit trusts do not normally charge another up-front fee for the transfer. Make sure you check before going ahead, however.

ADMINISTRATION COSTS

Many trusts have very little ongoing administration and you can generally do it yourself. Some do not even have a bank account. If you establish a trust where the only asset is the family home, you do not need IRD registration and there is no requirement for annual tax returns. Trusts do not need to be registered (unlike companies), so there are no annual return costs.

Of course, even the simplest of family trusts will need to be managed well and have a good paper trail. This means record-keeping, and, just because a trust is small and simple, there is no escaping the Trusts Act. The Trusts Act will see more costs for most trusts, including simple ones.

In the event that you wish to sell your house and buy a new one, someone will need to deal with real estate agents, and with financiers if there is a mortgage. Almost always, however, you will do this work yourself and present it to the trustees for agreement and signing. You should keep your trustees informed throughout the process, though, and always bear in mind that any decisions must ultimately be made by the trustees.

However, trusts with more substantial and varied assets will require more administration. For example, shares or unit trusts may need to be sold and new ones bought.

Similarly, government stock may be sold and new investments purchased. All of this may require some advice, and this may cost. On the whole, though, you can still do much of the spadework yourself. Charges by trustees who are professionals will generally be small if you have done most of the background work yourself. Some professional trustees may charge a percentage of the trust's assets or income for management. Discuss any likely costs before going ahead with anything, and agree the processes and management that will need to be done so that you ensure all of the trustee duties are performed properly.

Trading trusts (see Chapter 9) can require more work, depending on the number and the nature of the transactions. Most routine matters can be handled by you, with major transactions requiring the trustees to execute documents. Trustees who are professionals will usually charge on a time basis, and so it pays to do as much of the background work yourself as possible.

———

Q I want to put my home in a trust, but the bank has a mortgage over it to secure my company's overdraft. Can I still do it?

A Yes, you can, although the house will remain exposed to the bank. You will, however, gain some protection from unsecured creditors.

The way this would work is quite simple: the house would be transferred to the trust with the mortgage to the bank in place, and a guarantee is given by the trust to the bank for the company's overdraft. In the event of insolvency, the bank would still be able to get at the house but many of the other creditors would not.

It is a good idea to trade your business through a company and to give the bank a debenture over the company's assets. This would mean that, if you had business trouble, the bank would get paid out of the company's assets in priority to other creditors, meaning that it would need to get less (or perhaps nothing) out of the house.

6

Cost–Benefit: To Keep or to Wind Up?

If you are considering a trust you need to be very clear on the purpose or the benefit to you. Frequently I have heard stories where people have been told not to worry about why, just get on and do it. This carries on to a statement that everybody is doing it and you should join the rush. These exhortations to form a trust seldom come from professionals, but rather from friends, family, neighbours, etc., and, to say the least, are unhelpful. In fact, trusts are a very personal arrangement, and whether to form a trust or keep one that is already formed is an important, big decision — and it is most certainly not true that everybody will benefit from a trust today.

This also stands if you have already settled a trust, perhaps years ago: the benefit that you initially sought may have changed, or something within your life may have changed.

For example, you may have settled a trust because you had gone into business and you wanted to protect your lifestyle assets. Now you are no longer in business, and so that benefit is no longer there. Change happens to both you and the rules regarding trusts, and this change may mean that a trust is no longer of benefit. That means that rather than simply going ahead and forming a trust, or blindly continuing with a trust, because 'everybody is doing it', you need to do a cost–benefit analysis of using a trust given your own personal and family circumstances.

The advantages and disadvantages of trusts are set out in Chapters 3 and 5. This chapter looks at the weighing of the advantages and disadvantages (cost–benefit analysis). This cost–benefit analysis is not simply performed when you are considering setting up a trust; it needs to be repeated at regular intervals while you have the trust, to take account of any changes in the legal and regulatory environment of trusts (taking away the benefit) or in your own personal circumstances.

This chapter also includes some comment regarding winding up a trust. The requirements contained in the Trusts Act mean there will be many people who decide to wind up their trusts, and this chapter lays out the process and the way that this is usually done.

Those who have already settled trusts need to consider the costs and cost implications of wind-up in the cost–benefit analysis. This is because the cost to wind up the trust may be an important factor in whether or not you continue with the trust. For example, for some people there may be tax consequences with winding up the trust, and so it may therefore be better to continue the trust simply to avoid incurring these costs.

Of course, the weighing of costs versus benefits will be individual for each person. The benefits that accrue from the trust will clearly be different for different people, but the costs may be as well. (Some people will be more capable of managing a trust themselves, while others will require — sometimes considerable — professional input and incur more cost.)

The weighing of the costs and the benefits needs to be done very carefully, and, although there could be cost savings if you wind the trust up, you will have to spend money to discontinue the trust and sometimes this outlay may be considerable. On the whole, the costs to wind up are better incurred sooner rather than later — if a trust is giving minimal or no benefit, most people would be better advised to go ahead and wind up the trust rather than delaying.

However, as noted above, the tax consequences may be very complicated (and they could be expensive) and this will be an area where many people will certainly need expert advice.

COST–BENEFIT ANALYSIS

In some ways a cost–benefit analysis is quite simple. You define the benefit that will or may accrue from the trust (possible rest-home subsidies, asset protection, tax benefits, etc.) and consider the costs of setting up a trust or continuing with a trust that you already have. Chapters 5 and 3 set out in more detail what both the costs and the benefits of a trust may be, and these will apply whether you are considering settling a trust or trying to decide whether or not to continue with a trust that you have already settled.

It is almost impossible for most people to do a cost–benefit analysis precisely with numbers. Although there are certainly benefits and costs which concern money, there are also benefits and costs on which you cannot put a price. Moreover, trusts often look to manage risk (e.g. relationship failure, business collapse), and these risks may or may not eventuate.

For example, if you settled a trust because you were in business or a profession and wanted to protect lifestyle assets, you need to consider the chances of business failure as well as the financial impact of that failure. It is hard (or impossible) to put precise figures on this. Moreover, in these circumstances you would need to assess the chances of the trust being effective in protecting the assets; for example, the Official Assignee might possibly attack the trust and successfully overturn it. Benefits may simply be peace of mind: a trust gives you a feeling of comfort that your assets are protected, and, of course, it is difficult to quantify the benefit of peace of mind.

Costs can be the same: although there will most certainly be monetary costs of managing a trust on an ongoing basis, it is difficult or nearly impossible to put a dollar value on concern and worry about good management. A trust does mean that you have another entity to manage, and so, as well as financial costs, there will be peace-of-mind costs as well. A trust is another entity to manage and consider within your financial affairs, and so adds to the complexity — how can you put a number on that?

You must also remember that you need to add the requirements of the Trusts Act to the scales. These will be added on the cost side, because the Trusts Act will probably give beneficiaries a greater chance of being able to prove a breach of trust. (Or, at least, beneficiaries will be more aware of their rights, and so more likely to try to bring some kind of action.) Moreover, there will almost certainly be greater costs to manage the trust in terms of your own time and charges from a professional trustee (a lawyer or an accountant). The requirements of the Trusts Act mean that professionals are also likely to be less willing to act as trustees, and they are likely to charge more for their services.

To some extent for those who have already settled a trust, the decision will depend on how well you have been managing the trust in the past. If your management of the trust has been exemplary, the Trusts Act may create very little extra work or concern for you. However, those who have been cutting corners, and who have failed to do many of the things that good trust management demands, will need to do a great deal of work to bring their trust management up to speed — and that will cost.

My own observations in my work as a financial adviser and presenting seminars suggests that there are very few people setting up trusts at the moment. Mostly this is because the benefits of trusts have been whittled away over the years, with the benefits now weighing much less heavily on the scales. Moreover, there has been a considerable amount of case law which, along with the advent of the Trusts Act, weighs much more heavily on the cost side of the scales.

There are few clients or others for whom I have recommended the settling of a trust lately, and there have been a great many who I have suggested could usefully wind up their trust.

In the coming years many people will discontinue their trusts. The advent of the Trusts Act will cause many professionals to contact their clients to discuss with them bringing their trust management into line with the Act. This will trigger discussions on whether the trust continues to be worthwhile, and I imagine a number of people will conclude that their trust is no longer worthwhile, and will decide to wind it up.

To summarise, the benefits of a trust are:

— asset protection for those in business

— greater likelihood of qualifying for residential care subsidies

— income tax advantages

— succession

— asset protection for relationship property

— education trust.

The costs of a trust are:

— costs to establish

— costs to manage

— the risk of attack by beneficiaries

— the risk of attack by others (e.g. creditors, the IRD, the MSD, etc.).

Neither of these lists will be complete — there could be other benefits and other costs according to individual situations. Ultimately, in the absence of being able to undertake the process strictly by numbers, this weighing process will be a matter of judgement.

Ideally you will seek some help from a professional, and, even more ideally, this professional will know you, your family, your goals and aspirations well.

There are supposed to be 450,000 trusts in New Zealand, and I believe that many of those would be best wound up. This could be an expensive process, but, if benefits are gone or reduced, it may well be a better idea to wind up rather than continue. After all, the cost of managing an ongoing trust will become greater, and these costs will continue for the life of the trust — which could add up to a great deal.

WINDING UP A TRUST

Winding up a trust can be as simple or as difficult as each of our personal circumstances. Sometimes it is very simple to terminate a trust, and there may be little cost involved. At other times it may be very complicated and there could be considerable costs, particularly when tax consequences are added to the mix. This section assumes that you have already done a cost–benefit analysis, and following this weighing up you have decided to go ahead and wind up the trust. Here are the main steps you and your professionals will have to undertake.

1. IF THE TRUST HAS HAD INCOME, YOU ARE GOING TO NEED TO HAVE A DISCUSSION WITH YOUR ACCOUNTANT.

This discussion is necessary first to discuss the cost–benefit analysis and to see whether, from your accountant's point of view, there is any benefit retaining the trust. The accountant will consider your overall affairs, and other options for the ownership of your income-producing assets.

You also need to discuss with your accountant the tax consequences of winding up the trust. The tax consequences could be complicated (and expensive), depending on circumstances and on what the trust has been doing. It could, in a number of instances, mean that you do not go ahead with the wind-up.

One of the most common expenses in the winding up of a family trust is depreciation recovered. Depreciation recovered will be relevant to those who have significant income-earning assets in their trust (e.g. rental property or farming assets), which over the years have been depreciated. Some assets can be depreciated for tax purposes, but, even though there is a book entry for the depreciation and tax is claimed, the depreciation is not 'real' (i.e. the assets do not really fall in value, and so are sold at a higher value than the value they have been depreciated down to).

If the assets are sold (or distributed to beneficiaries) at true market value, it may be that this value is above the value that they have been depreciated down to in the books. This triggers 'depreciation recovered', which comes into the accounts as income on which tax will need to be paid.

For some trusts (e.g. farming operations, rental property or other businesses), this depreciation recovered can involve substantial amounts of money, and it may be that you are not in a position to pay this at the present time. This may mean that you do not go ahead with the wind-up.

There are other areas that can generate a tax consequence:

— The 'bright line test'. If you have purchased a property within five years, you would have tax to pay on any gains.

— Distributing to overseas beneficiaries. This is a highly technical area which would require consideration from advisers.

Discussions with lawyers and accountants are critical if you are considering winding up a trust that has had income-earning assets.

Trusts that have owned simply the family home are unlikely to have any tax consequences on winding up.

At the same time that you are having a discussion with your accountant, you need to try to assess what the cost of doing accounts for the trust has been (and will be in the future). The winding up of a trust may save you money not only in the ongoing management of the trust, but also in the preparation of accounts for the trust, and in winding the trust up you will save these. These savings would reduce the cost side of the equation.

2. IF THE TRUST HAS DEBT, YOU WILL HAVE TO DEAL WITH YOUR BANK.

There are a wide variety of circumstances and situations in this regard:

— some trusts will have no debt

— some trusts will have a simple mortgage on the home

— some trusts will have multiple debts for a wide range of purposes (business, investment, rental properties and the family home), which may be in a number of different entities with cross-guarantees.

Again, and as so often is the case with trusts, this will come down to your own particular circumstances.

In any event, you will need to deal with the bank if there is debt. As a simple example, a trust may own the family home that is mortgaged with a home loan. This home loan may be arranged in one of two ways:

1. the trust has borrowed the money and the house is mortgaged accordingly

2. the home loan is in your own personal name, but the trust has given a guarantee which is supported by the mortgage over the property.

However the debt might be arranged, if the trust assets are secured and you are winding up the trust, you will need to have discussions with the bank to make sure it will be happy to lend to you personally rather than to the trust. It is most unlikely that this will be a problem for the bank, and generally this will be something that your lawyer would do as a matter of course in transferring the property from the trust to your own personal name. However, the bank will consider the lending afresh, and there will, of course, be a cost to you of transferring the property and the loan to you.

This is not something that can be left to the last minute, because if you are not in a position to repay the mortgage (which is most likely) you will need to continue with the mortgage but through a new borrower (probably yourself personally).

3. WINDING UP AND DISTRIBUTION

From a technical point of view this stage is relatively easy. The trustees agree to bring forward the distribution date and distribute assets to beneficiaries at your discretion. Generally, this will see assets being distributed to you, and when this is done the trust will have no remaining assets. Yet again this will vary according to individuals — some people may want to make distributions to children or grandchildren, although I suspect most people will simply distribute to themselves as beneficiaries.

With the trust now owning nothing, it effectively no longer exists. However, it is likely your lawyer will draw up a 'deed of wind-up'. This simply confirms that there are no assets in the trust and that the trust is discontinued.

Already lawyers and accountants are getting a good deal of practice at winding up trusts, and I think this is most likely to continue over the coming months and years. While many of the trusts to be wound up will be fairly straightforward, there will certainly be some which will be much more difficult.

Even without tax consequences, the winding up of a trust is likely to cost $2000–$3000, and possibly more, depending on the amount and nature of the assets that will need to be transferred from the trust to beneficiaries. Nevertheless, there may be more costs than this, as for some people it may be necessary for new wills to be drawn up.

While the formation of a trust is generally a fairly standard piece of work for lawyers and trust companies, the winding up of trusts may be significantly less so. This will mean a good deal of variation of costs, to take account of the many different circumstances within families. You will have to work through all of the costs associated with winding up, and place these costs on the scales of your cost–benefit analysis.

THREE QUESTIONS:

---

1. Do you still have a valid purpose for the trust — one that will give you and/or your family some benefit?

If no, wind up the trust.
If yes, continue the trust.

―――

2. Having weighed the advantages of the trust against the disadvantages, have you found that the advantages weigh heavier?

If no, wind up the trust.
If yes, continue the trust.

―――

3. Have you managed the trust well in the past, and, whether you have or not, are you committed to managing it properly in the future?

If no, wind up the trust.
If yes, continue the trust.

7

Management of Trusts

I f you want the trust that you have formed to be bullet-proof — unable to be successfully attacked — you must manage it well and comply with the Trusts Act. If trusts are successfully undermined, it is usually not because of the way in which they were formed, but rather the way in which they are managed.

Chapter 2 sets out the duties of trustees — both the mandatory duties and the default duties — as contained in the Trusts Act. These duties do not constitute a change to the way a trust should be administered, but rather sets them out clearly in one place. It was always expected that a trustee would know the terms of the trust, act in good faith, and act for the benefit of beneficiaries (and all the other duties that are required in the Trusts Act); it is just that now we have the duties clearly laid down in statute.

Two groups of people may attack your trust. First, outsiders may try to overturn your trust, denouncing it as a sham. These outsiders may be the IRD, the MSD, creditors, a spouse/ partner or an ex-business partner. Secondly, beneficiaries of the trust may attempt to overturn it.

These people may attack the trust and the trustees if the trust has not been managed properly — i.e. as a prudent person would manage it. After all, the assets of the trust are beneficially theirs, and they have a right in law to have them looked after properly — just as the trustees have an obligation in law to do so. To eliminate the risks of attack from either of these groups, you need to manage the trust well.

Good trust management starts with an acknowledgement and understanding that the assets in the trust are no longer your own. Even though you may be a trustee (and therefore one of the legal owners) and also a beneficiary (and therefore one of the beneficial owners), the assets are not yours alone. You cannot act solely in your own interests; you must also consider the other beneficiaries, and not damage their positions.

SHAM TRUSTS

Someone attacking a trust will usually attempt to do so by having it declared a sham. When you look at the literature, the descriptive language tells us that a sham trust:

— gives the appearance of creating rights

— has an intention to mislead

— gives the appearance, but not the intention of forming a trust

— has the appearance of creating an entitlement

— is just an individual under another guise.

Two things stand out here:

— there is only the **appearance** of a divestment of assets (you may have gone through the process — signed the documents, etc. — but there is no substance)

— the trust is simply your alter ego — the assets are still really your own, under the guise of a trust.

This is what someone attacking the trust will try to prove: you have only created an appearance of a trust, and the assets are really yours.

Remember that for a trust to be valid, three things must be certain:

— The certainty of **intention** to create a trust. The deed will of course record this intention when you create the trust. However, if after the trust has been formed your actions are such that it appears that you never truly intended a trust to be created, it can be successfully attacked. For example, if you do not involve all of the trustees in decisions, or if you treat the assets as if they were your own, someone could cite this as evidence of no real intention to create a trust. Your actions in the management of the trust may give away your real intentions.

— The certainty of the **assets** of the trust. Again the paperwork must be there: the assets should be listed in the trust's account or asset register. However, some people intermingle their own assets with those of the trust (usually because they are not fully aware that the trust's assets are not the same as their own assets).

For example, a new bedroom may be added on to the house which is owned by the trust. Several times I have seen people pay for the addition with their own money instead of advancing cash to the trust, which then pays the builders. Another example would be a property investor who sells a rental property to the trust but never gets around to having the tenants pay the rental to the trust's bank account — but instead simply banks the rent into a personal account. In this case, who really owns the rental property, the investor or the trust? Is the trust real, or just a smokescreen to hide the fact that the investor really owns the property? The IRD would want answers to these kinds of questions.

— The certainty of the **purpose** of the trust. Someone attacking the trust would want to show that you never had any intention of benefiting anyone else through the trust — it was always really intended for your own benefit. Remember that it may be someone whom you know very well (an ex-spouse or a business partner) who is attacking the trust. Note that it would not necessarily be a problem if all of the beneficiary distribution had been made to you: the trustees are quite within their rights to benefit whoever they choose whenever they choose. Problems arise when it is clear that the trustees have not even considered the other beneficiaries.

This is one reason why all trust experts say that there should be a meeting of trustees at least once a year: it is hard to claim that all beneficiaries have been considered if the trustees haven't even met to discuss the beneficiaries.

Your trust may also be attacked because it infringes relevant legislation. There is not only the Trusts Act, but many other statutes apply, including the Trustee Act 1956, the Property (Relationships) Act 1976, the Property Law Act 2007 and the Social Security Act 1964.

The state of the trust's finances may also leave it open to attack. For example, if management has been poor, all of the gifting may not have been completed. You need to bear in mind who may instigate an attack, how they may do so, and what the consequences are of a successful attack.

Trusts are also attacked by beneficiaries. In the future, the number of cases of disgruntled beneficiaries taking trustees to court and claiming breach of trust is likely to increase. It may sound unpleasant, but family trusts are family affairs and, as we frequently see in the media, families do fall out.

Beneficiaries claiming breach of trust will look at the duties of trustees as laid out in the Trusts Act and identify where trustees have not complied. The Act's requirement to give beneficiaries information will come with plenty of publicity. Beneficiaries will therefore be well aware of their rights, and this is bound to provoke more disputes.

Again, good trust management starts with the right attitude and requires good knowledge of the Trusts Act.

GOOD MANAGEMENT

It should be clear that those trusts that are badly managed are the most vulnerable to attack. The trust that you have settled has to be managed according to the assumption that the assets in it are not yours (or not solely yours, at any rate). Instead, you have to manage the trust as if the assets are someone else's (as, indeed, they are, in part).

This is what I call 'the friend's car syndrome'. If you borrowed your friend's car, you would (hopefully) look after it even more carefully than your own, and make sure that you gave it back in the same or better condition than that in which it was given to you. The trust's assets are not entirely yours, and you should look after them like a friend's car. Everything that you do in managing the trust should be consistent with looking after the property of others. I often hear people use a phrase like 'my family trust'. When I hear this, I think: it is not *your* family trust — no one owns it. It is true that the trustees are the legal owners, and the beneficiaries are the beneficial owners of the assets. However, just because you settled the trust and you are perhaps one of the trustees and beneficiaries, you are not the owner of the trust — it is not yours, and you should not treat it as such.

The Trusts Act supersedes all, but in past editions of this book I have set out six main pointers for good trust management. These are still relevant, and are:

1. INVOLVE ALL TRUSTEES.

The trustees control the trust (at least, they should), and they should therefore know what is going on and be well enough informed to make decisions. They should not have 'done deals' simply dropped on them (e.g. when you have sold the trust's house and you ask them to rubber-stamp the deal by signing the sale and purchase agreement).

Involve the trustees early, and keep them in the communications loop. They will not take you, the trust or their position as trustees seriously if they do not know what is going on.

2. HOLD ANNUAL TRUSTEE MEETINGS.

This may not be required by law, but trust advisers consider it essential for a well-managed trust.

The absence of meetings can be considered evidence that the trust is merely an extension of the settlor. A meeting does not need to be long, but it provides an opportunity for the trustees to turn their minds to:

— the state of the assets (e.g. maintenance of property)

— investment strategy

— financial position

— distributions to beneficiaries

— trust records

— gifting

— tax

— trustee changes.

An annual meeting is not a great imposition, but is a good time to review what is happening and make sure that everything is being done and properly recorded.

3. IDENTIFY ASSETS.

The trustees need to be sure that they know what assets they own and what their liabilities are. To this end, each year financial accounts will be prepared (for trusts which have income) or a statement of assets and liabilities drawn up (for trusts which do not have income). It is surprising how many trusts are not sure what their assets are. There was a case some years ago of a dispute between the Official Assignee and a trust whose settlor had gone bankrupt. The settlor of the trust claimed that a classic car was the trust's property, while the Official Assignee claimed that it was personal property (and therefore could be sold to pay creditors). Keep a very good paper trail of what the trust owns and owes — the intermingling of trust assets with your own is not a good idea.

4. INSURE THE TRUST'S ASSETS.

A prudent person insures valuable assets, and so a trustee should make sure that the trust's assets are always properly insured. You should make sure that the insurance policies are in the name of the trust and, as trustee, that they are renewed each year.

5. BRING IN EXPERTS WHEN NECESSARY.

A prudent person takes advice when necessary. As a trustee you are looking after the assets of others, and so some kind of eccentric investment approach is not appropriate. For example, you ought not to use someone else's money to buy 'penny dreadful' shares. If you do, you could easily be accused by the beneficiaries of damaging their position, or by outsiders of having an unusual investment approach — implying that you are managing the trust as if the assets were your own.

6. CONSIDER ALL BENEFICIARIES.

This does not necessarily mean that all beneficiaries have to receive a benefit — in fact, the same beneficiaries may continue to receive the only distributions that are made. However, it is important that you do not forget any beneficiary: you must turn your mind to them all and consider them before making a distribution.

KEEPING RECORDS

The Trusts Act obligates trustees to keep core trust information. Each trustee must personally hold a copy of the terms of the trust, but can rely on another trustee to hold other documents.

The records that you keep provide the necessary paper trail. The key document for record-keeping is the 'minute book', which records all of the decisions that have been made by trustees. Note that this is probably no longer a 'book' as it used to be in the past, as most of the documents will be stored electronically.

If you have a professional trustee (which I highly recommend), that trustee should use the office filing system to store all documents and have good back-up. The documents that you will keep include:

— the trust deed

— variations to the deed

— a will

— an enduring power of attorney

— a letter of wishes

— sale and purchase agreements

— advice received

— contracts

— mortgage documents

— expert advice (e.g. from a financial adviser)

— valuations

— certificates of ownership

— acknowledgements of debt

— gifting statements

— the trust's financial accounts (or statement of assets and liabilities)

— income and expenditure records

— tax documents.

It is very important to keep these documents safely backed up. You may at some point need to justify why an asset was sold into the trust at a certain price. You may not be believed if you say that you got a valuation at the time but have since lost it in some kind of computer crash.

8

Accounting for Trusts

Many trusts do not need to be accounted for. Trusts that have no income do not need to register with the IRD or produce accounts or financial statements. There are many trusts in New Zealand that have perhaps only the family home and/or some family heirlooms as their assets.

While some trusts need to produce a full set of accounts, those that own non-income-producing assets, like the family home, still do need to keep financial records. All trusts need to keep statements of assets and liabilities, as well as a record of their income and expenditure. Small trusts with no income do not escape this requirement, and need a register of their assets and liabilities updated every year.

Any trust that has an income-earning asset, however, needs to register with the IRD, file tax returns and produce financial statements, regardless of the source of the income — investments in shares, unit trusts or property, or ownership of businesses.

It is an easy process to register with the IRD and get an IRD number. It is the same as for a company, a partnership or an individual: you simply fill in a form. The only additional thing you need do is to provide the IRD with a copy of the trust deed, and the trustees' IRD numbers.

There is no charge for registration.

Some trusts, particularly trading trusts or trusts with non-residential investment property, need to register for GST as well. This applies if the trust is engaged in an activity with taxable income of over $60,000. A trust that owns only residential income-earning property would not need to register for GST, but a trust owning commercial (or non-residential) property with rents (including outgoings) over $60,000 must register.

The requirement to produce annual tax returns increases the administration (and probably the costs) of the trust, and it is for this reason that many people put only the family home or other non-income-producing assets into their trust. While such trusts require no accounting information, those with substantial income-producing assets may require a lot of accounting input.

The basic accountancy for trusts is no different from that for any other entity — companies, partnerships, sole traders and so on. If you have investment property or a business that you sell into the trust, the accounting will be little different from what you have been doing already and so you might continue to do it yourself.

But there are some tax differences between trusts and other business entities that will almost certainly require the skills of a suitably qualified and experienced accountant. It is important that this person is well versed in the taxation of trusts. The accountant will do the final tax work, allocate income, and produce and file the annual tax return.

It is my preference for clients with trusts or companies to do as much of the basic accounting work as possible themselves, producing good financial information that makes it easy for well-qualified accountants to apply their technical expertise in the final tax work.

While some of the finer detail and more technical aspects of the taxation of trusts is outside the scope of this book (and lies in the domain of an accountant), there are some more general points of which you should be aware.

TAX ON TRUSTEE AND BENEFICIARY INCOME

Any income of the trust after expenses have been deducted can be deemed either trustee or beneficiary income. The trustees have the discretion to choose which it should be, and the decision will likely be dictated by tax considerations or perhaps family circumstances.

Income that remains with the trustees (i.e. trustee income) is treated similarly to company income: there is a flat tax rate of 33 per cent (for companies it is a flat rate of 28 per cent). The tax rate is applied to income after the deduction of allowable expenses, which are the same for trusts as they are for other business entities. These may include interest on borrowings, professional fees, depreciation, management charges, wages, and repairs and maintenance.

If, however, the trustees choose to divert income to the beneficiaries, this income is taxed differently. Income to beneficiaries over the age of 16 is taxed at the rate of 10.5 per cent up to $14,000, 17.5 per cent from $14,001 to $48,000, 30 per cent from $48,001 to $70,000, and 33 per cent thereafter. This beneficiary income is not quite the same as the personal income of the beneficiaries, in that some rebates cannot be claimed.

The lower rate of tax for each beneficiary is the reason why trusts are occasionally attractive for income splitting, as discussed previously. A family with children over 16 years who have no other income can achieve considerable tax savings in this way.

All income deemed to be beneficiary income has to vest absolutely in the beneficiary or be paid or applied to the beneficiary during the income year or within six months of the end of the income year.

The income need not be paid in cash, but can be credited to a loan account in the name of the beneficiary. At this point the funds are absolutely the beneficiary's and cannot be claimed back by the trustees. At age 18, a beneficiary can demand payment of any loan account.

The ability to divert income to a beneficiary within six months of the end of a financial year is important. This allows time for a trust with income to produce a set of accounts and allocate income in the most tax-efficient manner.

The trust is liable to pay income tax on any income going to the beneficiary, as it is deemed to be the beneficiary's agent. In practice, the trust will generally withhold tax on any income credited to the beneficiary, and so pay or credit the net income to the beneficiary. If the gross income were paid to a beneficiary who then failed to pay the tax, the trust could be liable for the unpaid tax.

Income is deemed to be taxable in the income year to which it relates, notwithstanding the fact that the beneficiary may not become entitled to it until the trustees resolve its allocation.

It is generally accepted by the IRD that, from a tax point of view, income undergoes no change by coming into the trustees' hands and then passing to the beneficiary. The income retains its character despite having passed through two separate entities.

A good example of this is income that has been derived from overseas, perhaps Australia. The income may have come from interest-bearing deposits there and would already have been taxed at 15 per cent. This would remain as partially taxed income, and would not therefore be fully taxed again. It can be paid to the beneficiaries with the 15 per cent tax credit.

TRUSTS FOR INVESTMENT

In New Zealand there is virtually no difference between companies and trusts at the income-derivation stage. Both have a flat rate of tax (33 per cent for trusts, 28 per cent for companies), and both can claim the same expenses and deductions. Similarly, because New Zealand has an imputation system, profits can be distributed from both companies and trusts with no further tax, provided that the trust or the company has already paid tax on the income.

However, trusts have an advantage with the distribution

of capital profits from the sale of investments. If a company owns an investment (for example, a property) and sells it at a profit, that profit goes to the company, not its shareholders. Although the company may have made a large tax-free capital profit, it may struggle to be able to distribute it tax-free to its shareholders. The company may need to buy back its shares or be wound up with any assets distributed to the shareholders in this way. In many circumstances this can be impractical, and it is a rather extreme way of getting capital profits out.

A trust has no such problems. If it sells a building or other investment and makes a capital profit, it can simply distribute the profit as capital to any beneficiaries. In the event someone other than a beneficiary is thought by the settlor to be worthy of receiving some of these capital profits, that person can usually be appointed a beneficiary and then receive his or her share.

THE INCOME TAX ACT 2007

The Income Tax Act 2007 contains the general anti-avoidance sections. These are one of the IRD's main weapons against tax avoidance, and allow any arrangement a taxpayer enters into, whose purpose or effect is to minimise tax, to be voided.

The important thing is that any arrangement must have a good commercial purpose: the minimisation of tax should be an incidental benefit rather than the principal purpose. Without these legislative constraints, it would be extremely easy to devise schemes and arrangements that would reduce or eliminate a taxpayer's obligations.

The Act's anti-avoidance provisions are seldom used by

the IRD against trusts. There are so many reasons for the establishment of a trust that it can be easily argued that any reduction in tax is a vicarious benefit.

One interesting use of the anti-avoidance provisions against trusts is the *Hadlee* case, which is discussed later in Chapter 9, where there was an assignment of personal income. The Privy Council effectively allowed the Commissioner of Inland Revenue to void Hadlee's arrangement, which had involved the assignation of his income as an accountant to the trust, enabling him to split that income among his family. This ruling, which prevents personal services income from being diverted, affects many people. Certainly, professional advisers (such as lawyers and accountants) are caught by this ruling. So, too, are wage and salary earners. There is also a grey area here: for example, does a plumber earn income by being in business or through performing personal services? If in doubt, it may be wise to seek a binding ruling from the IRD.

PIE REGIME

The PIE (Portfolio Investment Entity) regime concerns people, trusts and companies who invest in managed funds. The most common PIEs are KiwiSaver funds. Although trusts cannot invest in KiwiSaver funds (they are only for individuals), there are many other managed funds which are PIEs.

Under the PIE regime, managed funds are taxed at a special rate according to each member's income. The managed fund pays tax on your behalf, but you have to give the fund your Prescribed Investor Rate (PIR). Provided you give the fund the correct PIR, the tax that the fund pays for you is a final tax and, as a managed fund investor, you do not have to include the PIE income in your tax return.

The top rate for PIE managed funds is 28 cents. This is lower than the rate for trusts, and also lower than the top rate for beneficiaries who may be on a rate of 33 cents or 30 cents, respectively.

Trusts that have investment portfolios will often, therefore, get a tax benefit if they invest in a managed fund which is a PIE. The tax saving between the usual trust rate of 33 cents and the 28-cent rate for PIE managed funds can be quite significant. It may, therefore, be worth trustees considering making investments through managed funds rather than directly. (Note, though, that other factors like fees and investment performance also come into the equation.)

PENNY AND HOOPER

The Penny and Hooper tax case went right through the New Zealand court system, culminating in a decision in the Supreme Court in August 2011. Mr Penny and Mr Hooper were two Christchurch surgeons in private practice. Their practice was owned by a company, the shares of which were owned by family trusts. Mr Penny and Mr Hooper paid themselves artificially low salaries ($120,000 p.a.), which meant that only a relatively small amount of tax was paid at the top marginal rate (39 cents, at the time). The balance of the profits was passed through *as dividends to their respective family trusts, which were taxed at the lower company and trust rates. The cash from these profits was still available to the surgeons as distributions from the family trusts.*

The ownership structure that Mr Penny and Mr Hooper had in place was quite common — however, the Supreme Court found against them. The Court said that the tax advantage was one of the principal purposes and effects of the low salaries and ownership structure. This ruling has had ramifications for many people who have similar ownership structures and who also pay themselves low salaries for tax purposes.

———

Q I formed a trust four years ago but have never put any substantial assets into it. Should I use it?

A Before doing anything, get the trust arrangement checked out to make sure it contains all the provisions that most modern trust deeds have. Some older deeds are not as good or as flexible as more up-to-date ones. If this is the case, you would be far better off winding up that trust and starting again with a new one. Obviously, that will cost you money, but some expense now is better than a lot of trouble later on. However, assuming the trust deed is reasonably up to date, and has the provisions that are usual today, you can sell assets into the trust as it stands.

———

9

Parallel Trusts and Trading Trusts

Parallel trusts and trading trusts are types of family trusts. They are simply put together in a slightly different configuration to achieve particular ends. Like most family trusts, parallel trusts and trading trusts are usually discretionary, and all the usual rules regarding family trusts apply.

PARALLEL TRUSTS

Parallel trusts have grown out of mirror trusts. Mirror trusts were originally used by people who were concerned about avoiding estate duties. Under the Estate and Gift Duties Act 1968 anyone who was the settlor of a trust could not take any benefit from it — they had to be specifically excluded as a beneficiary. Thus it wasn't possible to put assets into a trust and take a benefit from them. The solution was for both the husband and the wife to set up a trust, each of which was mirror of the other: insofar as the husband was a beneficiary of the trust that the wife had settled, and the wife the beneficiary of the trust that the husband had settled.

Mirror trusts are now uncommon. More common today is a very similar form of trust arrangement called a parallel trust. The principle behind parallel trusts is much the same as for mirror trusts, the primary difference being that with parallel trusts the settlor remains a beneficiary (or at least a potential beneficiary) of both trusts. Because estate duties have gone, there is no need for the settlor to be specifically excluded as a beneficiary, although, if there were a change in the law, the settlor may have to exclude him- or herself once again.

I don't know who invented the idea of mirror trusts, but it proved to be a clever way of circumventing a very inconvenient piece of law. Mirror trusts provide a means of keeping the parties in the trust separate — having everything on an arm's-length basis. Parallel trusts do the same thing. It is for this reason, and because of the possible vulnerability of family trusts that are not at arm's length, that I am still in favour of parallel trusts for some people.

What you do is form not one trust, but two. The husband and wife each forms a trust, each one paralleling or mirroring the other in its terms. (Note that these scenarios apply to anyone in a relationship in terms of property law, but for simplicity's sake we will here refer to the parties as 'husband' and 'wife'.) The husband establishes a trust of which he is the settlor, and has a deed drawn up and executed. He appoints trustees and, in the case of mirror trusts, specifically excludes himself from any benefit under the trust — although with a parallel trust he might be a beneficiary or might retain the ability to be appointed a beneficiary in the future. The beneficiary of his trust (if he is not one himself) is his wife and very often their children.

The wife does exactly the same, generally appointing the same trustees. Diagrammatically a parallel trust looks like this:

Often the husband will be a trustee of the trust he has settled, while the wife will be a trustee of her trust. It is possible for each to be a trustee of the other trust; but, to keep the arrangement as separate as possible, it is better for outside people to be appointed as trustees.

Once the trusts have been established there comes the issue of the ownership of assets. This can be arranged in one of three ways:

1. Each trust can own separate assets. This involves a division of the relationship property with each trust owning certain assets. Thus the husband's trust might contain the house, antique furniture and art, while the wife's trust contains the holiday home, business assets and investments. Each trust would independently own assets which at the start would probably be of roughly equal value.

2. Each trust can own 50 per cent of each of the assets. In this way the wife's trust owns half of the house, half of the investments, half of the business and so on, while the husband's trust owns the other half. The problem with this form of ownership is double administration. Assuming that there is a business or other assets with income placed in the trusts, both trusts will have to register with the IRD and produce annual accounts. This obviously increases the administration and associated costs.

3. The two trusts can form a partnership to own all assets as partners. This means that the assets are owned by only one entity, which is the partnership of the two trusts. This is probably the most common way for parallel trusts to own assets, as the only comprehensive annual accounts required are for the partnership, not for the individual trusts. The

asset-owning entity would probably end up being called something like the Hawes Family Trust Partnership.

ADVANTAGES

Parallel trusts have two primary advantages. The first is that they can greatly simplify financial arrangements in the event of a marriage or relationship break-up. Depending on how the trusts own the various family assets, the usual arguments in the case of divorce might be avoided. If each trust owns its own assets, each partner may simply walk away with the assets he or she is entitled to as beneficiary of the other's trust. So if the house is in the husband's trust, the wife would take that (because she is the beneficiary), and the investments that were in the wife's trust would become the property of the husband as beneficiary under that trust.

Clearly, considerable thought would need to have been put into the ownership of the various assets before they were transferred into the trusts. While it is never pleasant discussing the possibility of a marriage break-up with a couple to whom the idea has never occurred, it is something advisers frequently find necessary or prudent.

As well as ensuring that the various assets put into the two separate trusts amount to a similar value, you need to make sure the terms of each of the trusts are equivalent. Particularly important is the right to remove and appoint trustees.

In this regard it is a good idea to have the husband act as appointor (the person who can hire and fire trustees and appoint or remove beneficiaries) of his wife's trust, while the wife is the appointor of the husband's trust. In that way the husband can, if necessary, appoint himself or other friendly trustees to the trust of which he is the beneficiary, and his wife can do the same for the other trust. In the event of a marriage break-up each can quickly appoint their own trustees so that they can take control of the trust from which they are going to benefit.

The other advantage of parallel trusts is that they provide a method of keeping all the parties separate, which could prove very beneficial in the event of any legislative change aimed at preventing settlors from benefiting from their trusts. If the law changed so that you could not be a beneficiary of a trust that you had settled, it should be an easy matter to remove you and your spouse as beneficiaries of your respective trusts.

Parallel and mirror trusts have been around for some considerable time, and as such are somewhat less likely to be attacked by any future law change.

DISADVANTAGES

The major disadvantage of parallel trusts is that they cost more and require more administration. Two trusts have to be formed, with two deeds drawn up and executed, and a partnership agreement may also need to be drawn up. However, given that the two deeds are identical in everything except the naming of beneficiaries, one trustee and the appointor, the set-up cost is unlikely to be double the cost of a single trust.

Any additional ongoing cost is likely to be small, as each trust would have the same management in terms of the Trusts Act; an extra few hundred dollars seems very little if it means that your arrangement is put together correctly. There may be more administration and compliance costs, depending on how the assets are owned. If each trust individually owns income-producing assets, financial accounts will need to be done for both. The burden of this requirement is alleviated, however, if the two trusts form a partnership that owns all the assets. In this event it is only the partnership that needs financial accounts, although both trusts must still file tax returns.

SUMMARY

When estate duties were abolished in December 1992, many advisers dropped the use of mirror trusts. Indeed, some advised that mirror trusts should be unwound and the assets resettled onto a new single trust.

However, I take a contrary view. I believe that people who already have mirror or parallel trusts should (all else being equal) retain them, and couples who are thinking of establishing a trust should consider having parallel trusts. This may mean something of a debate with your lawyer or other adviser. But remember that it very often pays to not do what everybody else is doing. It is true that there is currently no piece of law that says that you cannot be settlor, trustee and beneficiary of a trust, and most single trusts are formed along these lines. But such an approach may prove to be short-sighted.

Given the advantages (and lack of significant disadvantages) of mirror or parallel trusts, they are at least worth considering as a vehicle.

TRADING TRUSTS

A trading trust is in nearly every respect a standard family trust. The only difference is that it actively pursues business profits. A trading trust holds business assets, and trades just like a company, partnership or individual. A major benefit of this is usually income splitting, as described in Chapter 3.

The assets held by a trading trust are those typical of any trading concern or business. The trust actually owns the business and its assets — plant and equipment, debtors, stock, property and leases.

Although a trust may hold shares in companies that carry on a business, the income from these may not achieve the aim of income splitting. The shares that the trust might hold in the company will produce dividends that are in effect already taxed (imputed). The aim of a trading trust is often to have before-tax income available to the trustees to distribute to beneficiaries.

Any type of business may be traded by a trust except one that has income from an individual's own personal exertion. This last type of income is deemed to be personal income, and as such cannot be assigned to the trust. The Income Tax Act 2007 precludes accountants, for example, from channelling their income to a trust to be split among the beneficiaries.

This ruling was confirmed years ago, when the *Hadlee* case went all the way to the Privy Council. In 1993, the Privy Council found against Hadlee (a Christchurch accountant) and spelled out that there could be no effective assignment of personal services income from an individual or a partnership to a trust.

Most businesses can quite satisfactorily be traded through

a trust. Trusts owning more usual businesses (e.g. retailers, transport operators, manufacturers and so on) are not common but are by no means rare. In some instances, too, the 'personal services' income-earning aspect of a practice can be separated out from the assets of the trust. For example, the building and/ or equipment of a medical practice is owned by a trust and rented to the doctor or dentist. This rent is assessable income to the trust, and is often split among family members to utilise lower rates of tax.

Very often trusts hold income-producing property, the rent from which can be shared out among the beneficiaries. Many farmers have put their farms into trusts. Generally the land and buildings will be put into the trust, while the farmer will continue to own the stock and plant. The farmer then leases the land from the trust, which means that income (the rental) goes to the trust, and can be split for tax purposes among family members.

ADVANTAGES

As previously described, the primary advantage of a trading trust is the ability to split income among beneficiaries. When choosing a particular type of entity to own your business (be it a company, a partnership or a sole trader), the ability to split income among different members of the family (thus attracting lower tax rates) is one of the most important tax-planning tools. As noted in Chapter 3, this is subject to the rules against minors — those who are under 16 would have to pay tax at the top rate.

If you trade through a limited liability company you might be able to channel income to your spouse quite easily. Provided both shareholders are directors of the company, directors' fees can be paid and, although one spouse's role in the company may be greater than the other's, it is usually possible to justify some sort of salary for the shareholder-employee who works less.

However, a company structure does not easily allow you to split significant income to children who have no other income. While income may be paid to children for jobs like mailbox drops or updating the business's Facebook page or website, such amounts will necessarily be small. To take maximum advantage of income splitting you may want to pay out up to $48,000 to each child who is over 16, but this might be difficult to justify.

These problems do not exist if the business is held by a trust. The trustees have complete discretion as to which beneficiaries will receive income and in what proportion. They do not need to justify in any way a payment to a beneficiary in terms of work done. This makes a trust an ideal vehicle for income splitting. Note, however, as mentioned previously, income distributed to children who are under 16 years of age will be taxed at 33 cents.

DISADVANTAGES

There are two disadvantages many people see in trading their business through a trust, but both are fairly easily overcome.

Loss of limited liability

Companies do provide some measure of protection for shareholders and directors. The fact that companies have limited liability is one of the main reasons why people use them as their trading entity.

When dealing with the creditors of the business, personal trustees (i.e. trustees who are 'natural persons') will not have their personal liability limited unless they make it clear to the supplier at the time of order or supply that they are acting as trustees and agree with the supplier that their liability is limited to the assets of the trust.

The situation will therefore need to be explained to each of your suppliers and creditors. Without such explanation and agreement, the trustees' liability will be personal and unlimited. (Almost certainly a trustee would have an unlimited personal liability for any unpaid taxes, however.)

The appointment of a company as trustee means that the liability of the settlor and family members is limited (although that of the directors of the company may not be). If both the assets and the liabilities are held in the name of a company as trustee, any liabilities are limited to the capital of the company. There may be no personal liability.

The Companies Act 1993 extended considerably the duties and obligations of directors, so there could be some personal liability for the directors of corporate trustees if they did not fulfil their duties properly. However, this is the same in all respects as if you were trading your business through a company rather than through a trust with a company as trustee. A trust with a company as trustee would find itself in much the same position in the event of insolvency or financial difficulties as a business simply being traded through a company. Creditors who remained unpaid would initiate action against the company to get at the assets that the company held. In the case of a trust, the company would be holding the assets in trust, but these assets would in the first instance be available for creditors.

For this reason you should ensure that you do not have other lifestyle assets in your trading trust. If you have a trading trust to run your business, don't put the family home into the same trust or you run the risk of losing it to creditors. You may well need two trusts — one for business assets and one for non-risk family assets.

Lack of corporate identity

Your family trust may be known as the John Smith Family Trust but you want your business to be known and recognised as John Smith Panelbeaters Ltd. This problem is also easily overcome, this time by the use of a corporate trustee. The company that you have as trustee would be named John Smith Panelbeaters Ltd, and as trustee it would enter into all of the usual business arrangements with suppliers, customers, etc.

The business would thus become known as John Smith Panelbeaters Ltd, and, given that trust deeds do not need to be registered, no one would know (or indeed need to know) who were the final beneficiaries of the assets and the income.

MANAGEMENT OF THE TRUST

The assets of a trading trust are held by the trustee, and the trustee deals with them. However, day-to-day management of the trust would continue to fall on you in much the same way as before. It could be that a management contract is drawn up between you and the trust, or the trust might pay you a salary as manager.

It is likely that you would be the signatory on the bank account just as before, and would continue to do all the things you have done since you had the business.

The major difference in a management/administration sense is that major sales or purchases of assets or anything involving banking facilities would need to be executed by the trustees — in this case, the company. However, these major arrangements are usually infrequent.

It is important to be aware that assets in trading trusts tend to be at risk from the vagaries of the economy and the business cycle. Most business people want to protect their house (and holiday home or other lifestyle assets) in the event of business failure, so these assets should be quarantined off (perhaps in a separate trust) from the business trading entity.

———

Q Is there a downside to putting the shares of the company that owns my business into a trust?

A Yes, there is. A trust can own shares in companies, but this may not enable you to split income, because the profits of the company can only be transferred to the trust as tax-paid dividends. The profits of the company will be taxed in the company (at 28 per cent), and the dividends will therefore go to the trust imputed. Because the profits are already taxed in the company, there may be no advantage for you splitting them to try to get lower tax rates. There may be ways around this for some people, but this is something that requires input from an accountant.

10

Practicalities

There are many legal, technical and accounting details that are essential to the proper establishment of a trust — indeed, far more than are contained in this book. Much of this detail should not be of particular concern, provided you obtain good advice from both an accountant and a lawyer before and during the formation of your trust. You do need to know, however, about some of the practicalities surrounding trusts and their operation.

In some ways the Trusts Act 2019 makes managing a trust simpler: the things that you have to do are now clearly set down in one piece of law.

ADMINISTRATION OF A TRUST

The management and proper administration of a trust is very important, as you will have seen throughout this book and particularly in Chapter 7. The assets contained in most trusts continue to be managed largely by the settlor. If you have established a trust and transferred the family home into it, you will likely continue living there. You will also (probably) continue to mow the lawns, maintain the property and pay the rates and insurance. (The requirement for you to do this should be well documented.) Management of the trust's property continues just as it did before you transferred it.

A similar situation usually exists with other assets. If investments such as shares, unit trusts, bonds or interest-bearing deposits are transferred to the trust, the primary decisions regarding buying and selling are likely to remain with you. You will probably look after these investments in much the same way as you did before, but the trustees will sign any transfers when buying or selling. This does, of course, mean that the trustees have ultimate control and so you should be very sure to involve them.

Of course, a prudent person takes advice when needed, and a trustee is required to act as a prudent person. This may mean that, in order to avoid future conflict or claims of breach of trust from beneficiaries, you seek more investment advice for investments. I would argue that investment advice is nearly always a good idea, and this is especially so when you are acting as trustee.

Assets such as investment property and businesses will also probably be managed by you. In many instances the settlor looks after the investment property in all respects, even to the extent of being a signatory on the bank account and therefore managing all of the day-to-day running. It is most likely the trustees will follow your recommendations as to the management of assets, both in terms of buying and selling (major strategic decisions) and daily administration.

Some people form trusts, place investments in them, and require the trustees or a professional manager to make the major investment decisions. It is reasonably common for people to form a trust and to allow, say, one of the major trustee companies to invest and control their assets. This happens particularly when the settlor is incapacitated or perhaps has no particular skill, aptitude or inclination for investments. Professional managers will of course charge for this service — typically a percentage of the assets under management, or on a time basis.

Assuming that you are to continue managing the trust's assets yourself, you will still require the trustees to agree and to sign documents relating to the sale or purchase of assets. It is therefore important that you have trustees who are sympathetic to your aims, and that you keep them well informed. It is also important that your trustees are readily available.

Many trusts (for example, those that own the family home) will have very few transactions. If yours is like this, you may require little service from your trustees. Trusts that buy and sell shares or invest and trade in property may require ongoing discussions, and regular trustee approvals and signatures. This will result in some charge from the trustees, particularly if they are professionals (lawyers, accountants or trustee companies).

BANKS

It is very common for trusts to borrow from a bank and require other banking facilities. Indeed, probably the only trusts that do not require the services of banks are those that hold the family home or any other non-income-producing assets that are mortgage-free. However, even these trusts may have bank accounts unless there is clear agreement that you will pay all costs on behalf of the trust.

Banks tend to treat trusts and companies in a similar manner. To open a bank account or obtain some facility you will need to supply the bank with a copy of the trust deed. The bank and the IRD are the only bodies that are likely to require your trust deed, and of course both will keep the deed and its terms confidential.

When a trust borrows from a bank (be it a mortgage for the family home or an overdraft facility for a trading trust), the trustees take on the liability in their own names. The bank will generally agree to limit the liability of any independent trustees to the assets of the trust, and a clause will be inserted in the loan and mortgage documentation to this end.

The bank will most likely require a personal guarantee from you as settlor — although I have seen a few instances of banks missing this requirement — just as the directors of a company usually personally guarantee the company's banking facilities. Apart from this, your trust should be able to obtain finance on the same terms and conditions as an individual, a partnership or a company. In other words, normal banking criteria should apply in terms of securities provided, ability to service, cash flow and so on.

There is no legal reason why you as settlor cannot be a

signatory and operate the trust's account, although this does give the appearance of a very close relationship and too much control, and so it is not recommended. For trusts with very few banking transactions it is probably preferable to have the trustees as the only signatories. For example, a trust with only a mortgaged family home would see probably only two or three transactions a month. Most of these would probably relate to the mortgage repayments and could be managed by automatic payment.

Trusts with a greater number of assets and more activity may require many transactions each month, and it may not be practical to have to go to the trustees each time you need a cheque signed. In such cases it might be desirable for the trustees to hold the bank account and pay accounts each month.

Still, I know a number of trusts where the settlor manages the trust and operates the bank account independently of the trustees. If you prefer this, it is necessary to draw up a formal management contract between you and the trust, allowing you to manage the trust's assets on a day-to-day basis under the supervision of the trustees. You could then have your own account operating as the manager of the trust. Although such a structure may seem more practical, to me it seems far better to have the trustees operate the bank account if it can be managed without too much inconvenience.

Q If I form a trust, will I need to make a new will?

A Quite probably — the creation of a trust does change your financial position, and it is also a good opportunity to review your will.

Many people change their will so that all of their assets go into the trust. This includes any of the debt that remains at the time of their death, which effectively writes off the debt. Your will can also nominate the people who are to be trustees (and appointors) after you have gone.

II

Last Word

If you have battled through this book and got this far, you certainly have an interest in family trusts! This interest may be that you are thinking of setting up a family trust or, perhaps more likely given the advent of the Trusts Act, you are thinking of winding up a trust that was settled some time previously. Either way, you will have to carefully weigh the benefits of trusts against the costs — and then come to a decision.

I expect that this decision will be made with the help of an expert. I have noticed in recent months that lawyers have been writing to their clients and telling them about the Trusts Act and the likely implications for the way that trusts are managed. That is a good thing and something that is likely to increase.

Over the 25 years since it was first published, I have been told by many lawyers and accountants that this book played a big part in many trusts being formed in New Zealand — it was one of the reasons that New Zealand has more trusts per capita than any other country. This may be so, and it may also be so that the book now plays its part in seeing many trusts disestablished. If this is correct, the book mirrors the conclusions and activities of lawyers: they were busy forming trusts a few decades ago, and now will be busy winding them up.

I never really envisaged this and, indeed, did not expect so many trusts to be formed. Moreover, I did not expect a lot of trusts to be established where there was never much likelihood of the settlors getting much benefit. However, I have heard of (and, many times, I have met) people who have formed trusts with little or no due cause — they did it simply because it seemed the thing to do. These people had no clear purpose for a trust, but had gone ahead with a trust because everyone else was doing it.

I have only a little sympathy for most of these people. Although there are probably some who were sold trusts by overzealous professionals looking for work, I have heard many anecdotes from lawyers regarding people who demanded the establishment of a trust and would brook no argument.

Of course, there may be people who have had no benefit and are quite grumpy about being told that they should now wind up the trust (more cost!). I have a recently retired friend who spent his life in business. He established a trust in 1997 because he was always fearful of insolvency and he wanted to protect the house for his family. He now complains that he has spent good money forming a trust and managing it, but received no benefit. My response is that he is looking at things the wrong way. The fact is that it is a good thing that he has never had a benefit from the trust: it means he never became insolvent, which surely is preferable to becoming insolvent and getting a benefit from the trust's safety net. I asked him if he would prefer his house to burn down, so he could make a profit on his home and contents insurance. Like insurance, you pay a cost for a certain protection, but you still hope that the event from which you are protecting yourself does not happen.

I know that the weighing of risks and cost is a difficult thing for most people. There are unknowns on both sides of the scales: unknown costs and unknown risks. This is not a precise science.

The Trusts Act will probably raise the stakes. It could be that as more beneficiaries are given details of trusts, potentially more family arguments will arise, with children making claims on their parents' trusts. To avoid such dissension, there will certainly be people who decide to wind up their trusts so that they do not have to disclose their finances to wider family members.

On the other hand, I know that many people will continue with their trusts. They may need to smarten up the management, and this may cost, but many will perceive the benefits to be worth the cost.

In the final analysis, if you are struggling to decide whether to continue or not, you are probably best to keep the trust going for a while longer. This is effectively erring on the conservative side — you will have to do some work to make sure that the trust is well managed, but there is probably less cost to that than winding up the trust and then later regretting it. After all, in a couple of years you can always wind up the trust, but, if you discontinue it now, in a couple of years you cannot bring it back to life. For at the end of the day, there is a good reason why the trust vehicle has endured for centuries: a well-thought-out, structured and managed trust can provide families with great solace and security and embodies both surety and flexibility in responding to changing times.

Index

A

B

C

R

S

T